IVA.co.uk: Real Life IVA Stories

Real life tips from the largest online IVA community in the UK

by Andy Davie

IVA.co.uk: Real Life IVA Stories

Copyright © 2008 by IVA.co.uk

Published by IVA.co.uk

Cover design by Mike Andrews

All rights reserved. No part of this book may be reproduced of transmitted in any form or by any means without the written permission of the publisher.

First edition

ISBN 978-0-9558575-0-8

Acknowledgements

My thanks go to lovely wife, Beverly who has stood by me through thick and thin. Also our four children, Jason, Sean, Jasmin and Katie who have been endlessly patient and supportive.

Also thanks to everyone who helped bring this book to life, including Angela Pole, Melanie Giles, Mark Allen, Dominic Corby, James Falla, Jonathan Tinsley, Richard Reid, Julian Donnelly, Steve Rees, Jake Simons, Sara Smith, Stephen Parry and Tim Leach.

And finally, thanks to all the regular IVA.co.uk forum members who make IVA.co.uk what it is, especially angela18, chris.g, Soulgrowth, Viki.W, kallis3, emma_t, lily, Moneystinks, lesley_, ladyh, facingittogether, ray_a, debbiw, iva_squirrel, tracy.h, jpj, Sadsack, Dominic, Catullus, cr15py, olympic_torch, jane.l, caraf, dots, animaleyes76, mish1953, zoe, thebear29uk, cat 1, ThomasCharles, michael.t47, bagpuss, hara, pixie, DebtDummy, louisa.s, luluj, inaiva, wen, JulianSampson, BrassicLintus, pippa, debtfreesusie67, Martin2011, mikebdomain, iva.com, iva experts, Swans_girl, james.c, sblack, Beechy, plasticdaft, aguise, freelili, mrs skint, scaredkez, Barrington, Brett England, Skippy13, Mike Burridge, ianmillington, carlmcmullen, abc, Welsh Boy, Andrew Graveson, Storm, Clear Start, Mike Morgan, Cybus, Reviva UK, and CoverItAll.

Contents

Introduction	7
What is an IVA?	15
Chapter 1. The Debt Spiral	27
Chapter 2. Finding a solution	59
Chapter 3. Submitting an IVA proposal	91
Chapter 4. Making your IVA a success	125
Conclusion	162
Glossary	164

Introduction

My debt problems began when my business started to go wrong. I owned a small green grocer's shop in a little village in Bedfordshire, and I supplied all of the locals with their fruit and veg. I had fought my way out of debt once before. In the early nineties I had been caught up in the boom-and-bust property market and ended up with negative equity, three small children, a redundancy and £20,000 of unsecured debt. But I pulled myself out of it by taking the £14,000 redundancy money and buying myself the greengrocer's shop.

It was the best decision I ever made. Lots of the local people knew me already, and a customer base immediately began to spring up. There was always a steady stream of customers in the shop throughout the day, and they would always stop and chat as they chose their groceries. I loved being my own boss, and my enthusiasm attracted more and more customers. Before long the money came rolling in, and I bought a four bedroom detached house and a Mercedes with personalised plates. My family got used to two or three foreign holidays a year. We became known as the success story of the village and could hold our heads up high in the local pub.

A few years later, I tried to expand. I funded the expansion on credit cards in the hope that the other shops would enjoy the runaway success of the original. However, it didn't work out that way and the new shops just didn't take off. For a while I lived in the hope that things would pick up, that the satellite shops would begin making a profit and then I could pay off the credit cards. But sadly it never happened.

I remember the day when I finally accepted that things were falling apart. I drew up the blinds, allowing the morning light to enter the shop. It was a beautiful morning, one of the first days of spring, and I was feeling happy for a change. I was almost able to forget the pile of unopened letters at home. My bank balance was looking good; I had checked it that morning and found that I had a good £75 left between me and the overdraft limit – more breathing space than usual. Maybe I could put £20 on a couple of cards, just to keep them sweet.

The phone rang. It was unusual for somebody to call so early. I stepped behind the counter and pressed the receiver to my ear.

"Andy?"

"Rob, hi, how's tricks?"

Rob was the local fruit and veg wholesaler. I was always glad to hear from him. Although he was a business acquaintance, over the years we had struck up something of a friendship, doing each other favours and cutting each other slack when we needed it. Rob was a big, gentle man with honest eyes and a rolling laugh. He had grown up on a farm, and worked his way into the world of business when he was only eighteen. He was a good man – the sort of guy you could rely on.

"Andy…there's something I have to speak to you about, mate."

"Fire away."

"Well, it's your account. It's passed the ten grand mark, and rising every week. I hate to bring it up…"

"No, Rob, it's fine, thanks for telling me. I was just about to put some money your way, actually. I'll make sure you have a cheque by the end of the day."

"Thanks, Andy. Sorry to be a pain, it's just that I've never had someone owe me so much before…"

"No, Rob, it's nothing. Just an oversight, you know? The money will be with you by the end of the day."

As I replaced the receiver, my hand was shaking. It was like a bad dream coming back. This was the first time that Rob had ever mentioned my account arrears. Usually we operated on a kind of gentleman's agreement, him extending my credit as far as I needed it, and me paying it off as regularly as I could. And Rob hated talking about money. For him to ring me personally to chase up the debt must have meant he was seriously worried.

That was when it hit me. I was putting on a smile, but deep down my guts were churning. Things were not going to get better. They were steadily getting worse. I was in debt again, and this time it wasn't just twenty grand, it was sixty eight thousand pounds. I realised that I had been in denial.

"Sixty eight thousand pounds," I said out loud. "Sixty eight grand. Sixty eight grand." My voice had a strange, strangled edge to it. Sixty eight thousand pounds was a lot of money.

"I'm in denial," I thought to myself. And I was depressed, the night before I had only slept a couple of hours. I was lying awake, wondering what it would be like to be dead. "I'm in a bad way. These credit cards and loans are not going to just disappear by themselves. Something has got to be done."

But how would I tell Beverly? Last time we were in serious debt she was terrified that we would lose the house. I could see her in my mind's eye, her mouth going into that tight-lipped line that signifies severe stress. How could I break it to her this time? How could I tell her I'd done it again? And what would she say? Would she leave me?

I sat down on the stool behind the till, took my wallet from my pocket and let it fall heavily onto the counter. It flopped open, exposing row upon row of credit cards Visa, MasterCard, Gold, Platinum, Club, Diners, Premier and Switch. All gleaming, cheerful and ready to be used. I took a pair of scissors from the draw under the counter and slowly cut through them one by one.

That evening, after the children had gone to bed, I took a deep breath, got up and turned off the telly. My hands were shaking – I think they had been shaking all day.

"What did you do that for?" my wife asked sleepily.

"Darling, we've got to ... have a chat."

I swallowed, hard. My tongue was dry. I sat down next to her on the sofa. Bev looked at me suspiciously, her eyes full of concern. The last time when we had 'sat down and had a chat' our relationship nearly ended.

"What is it, love?" she asked. "What's up?" Already I could see her mouth forming the dreaded line. I opened my mouth, took a deep breath, and the whole story came tumbling out.

That was over four years ago. Now, as I sit here typing my story, it all feels like a distant memory. The main difference, of course, is that now I am debt-free. When my hard-earned money goes into my account every week, it's my own. I have no minimum payments to make, no balances to transfer, no loans to consolidate. I am totally clear of unsecured debt, and it feels great. Actually, it feels a little surreal after so many years of scraping together minimum payments and watching every penny. Now I can actually put money aside every month, something that not too long ago I could only have dreamed of. I still budget my spending carefully, of course, but now I appreciate what I've got, and so do my wife and children. When we go out for a meal, it's a treat. On Christmas, or on their birthdays, the children are genuinely grateful when they get a great present. Our lives have completely turned around, and the future, for once, looks promising.

All this is the result of the IVA that I did. When I finally admitted to myself that there was a real problem, I made some enquiries, spoke to some professionals, and eventually put together an IVA proposal, which was accepted. Four years on I have paid off what I can, and the rest has been written off. Of course that's fantastic, but it hasn't been an easy ride. The stress of being in debt is bad enough, let alone the anxiety that arises when you take your head out the sand and start looking around for debt solutions. And then there are all the sharks on the market - who do you trust? The banks? The Internet? The newspapers? The television? Everyone seems to recommend a different solution, everyone seems out to make a buck, and it's so hard to find a voice you can trust. That's why I got involved with IVA.co.uk, and that's why I'm writing this book.

IVA.co.uk

IVA.co.uk is the UK's biggest online IVA community, receiving over 5.4 million hits every month. In addition to providing expert advice and online access to IVA specialists, it features a live forum, free blogging space and an online TV channel providing a regular roundup of the latest news from the world of debt solutions. Since it was launched in 2005, IVA.co.uk has quickly become a leading online authority on UK debt and finance. More and more people are turning to the site for hard-to-find expert advice and to compare their experiences with others.

    Having been through the stress of an IVA myself, over the last couple of years I have been a regular contributor to the IVA.co.uk debt forum, helping people who were in the same position as I was find their way through the IVA jungle. I can see the stress they are under and the fear they are in as they post their questions – I've been there myself. I try to act as the voice of experience, guiding them as best I can through the IVA process and answering any questions they might have, along with the other experts that regularly post on the forum. IVA.co.uk has become a place where people can support each other through the stressful process of proposing an IVA. Most of these people are going through the same experiences I went through; they may be worried, confused, stressed, depressed, bewildered, suspicious and in desperate need of help.

As a result of my constant posting on the IVA.co.uk forum, I was asked to be the Site Manager and Spokesperson for IVA.co.uk in 2006, a position which I embraced wholeheartedly. It is such a meaningful experience to give people a helping hand when they are at rock bottom, and help them climb out of the hole, and I believe that I have something unique to offer people - personal experience. No matter how much a professional Insolvency Practitioner or debt advisor may try to help, they will never know what it is like to be in that level of debt. They will have no experience of the sleepless nights, the depression, the anxiety and the relationship strain that serious debt can cause. That is why the IVA.co.uk debt forum is so very popular; people can get advice and support from other people, real people, people who have gone through the massive test of proposing an IVA themselves, sticking to it, and coming out the other side.

This book

This book goes through the entire IVA process, including the origins of the debt problem, talking to friends and family, seeking professional advice and seeing through five years of budgeting. I will take the journey step-by-step, at each stage bringing in the contributions of other people who have gone through the process and expert advice from professionals. In this way, this book is your own personal IVA community, brought to life for you here on the page. I very much hope that it proves an invaluable resource as you contemplate taking the first steps towards solving your debt problems, and the light at the end of the tunnel.

What is an IVA?

IVAs have been around since the Insolvency Act in 1986, but surprisingly few people know much about them. An Individual Voluntary Arrangement (IVA) is a legal contract between a debtor and his or her creditors. The debtor agrees to make reduced payments over a fixed period, typically five years. After this time the debt is classed as settled, and any outstanding debt is written off.

Due to its formal nature, an IVA has to be set up by a licensed professional called an Insolvency Practitioner (IP). The IVA is a legally binding agreement designed to help those in financial difficulties settle their debts within a reasonable period of time.

The IVA is usually seen as a way to avoid Bankruptcy. When it is set up correctly, it provides an affordable payment plan and complete protection from creditors

What are the arrangements?

Monthly payments are based on your budget. After reasonable living expenses (rent, food, bills, clothing, travel and so on) anything you have left is what you offer the creditors. This is called your 'disposable income', and this is paid each month to your IP who will distribute it amongst your creditors. Any interest and debt charges will be frozen and creditors will be prevented from demanding additional payments. Once the final payment is made, usually after five years, any outstanding debt is legally written off. The arrangement can write off up to 70% of your debts, subject to your circumstances.

How does it work?

In order to propose an IVA, you will have to be able to offer to repay at least 30% of your original debt, usually over five years. For example, if you owe £50,000 in unsecured debt, you will have to be able to repay at least £15,000 of it, or 30p in the pound. You should note that some creditors have their own individual 'hurdle rates' – the minimum dividend they will accept before they approve an IVA. Your IP will be able to advise you about individual creditors, as well as the amount you should expect to repay.

If you have decided that an IVA is right for you, you will be asked questions regarding your current financial situation. Based on the information you give, a repayment amount will be agreed with you. This will typically take the form of sixty monthly payments (five years) of your disposable income. Once proposals have been drawn up you will need to check and sign these and return them to your IP.

The IP will then draft the IVA proposal and submit it to the creditors' accountants. A creditors' meeting will be convened and they will vote to either accept or reject your IVA proposal. If 75% of creditors accept the proposal, the IVA will be agreed. It is then legally binding upon all the creditors. You may be asked to attend your creditors' meeting, but this rarely happens. Normally you are asked to be contactable by phone on the day.

When an IVA is accepted the IP's role becomes that of supervisor, monitoring the IVA's progress and ensuring that the terms and conditions that were agreed to at the creditors' meeting are upheld. During an IVA, your financial situation will be reviewed regularly to see if there has been any change in your circumstances. It is the debtor's responsibility to pay the agreed payments to the IP who will then ensure that these payments are distributed to all creditors until the successful completion of the IVA. It is in the debtor's own interest to maintain their payments, as failure to pay will almost certainly result in the failure of the IVA.

Upon the successful completion of the IVA, the debtor will be considered debt-free, even though they may not have actually paid off all of their debts in full. Any outstanding balances are written off and the debtor is then free to make a fresh financial start.

It is worth noting that if you do enter into an IVA and you have a reasonable amount of equity in your property, then it is likely that most of it will have to be released at sometime during the arrangement so it can be paid to creditors in a lump sum. Drastic as this may sound, it can be a deciding factor in whether an IVA is approved by creditors and a realistic way in which a debtor can retain control of their property. Sometimes, an IVA can be proposed on the basis of equity release or other lump sum as a single payment. This is called a 'full-and-final settlement'. There is also an option of settling an IVA early if money suddenly becomes available to the debtor. This is called an 'early settlement'.

At the back of this book you will find a useful glossary of key terms related to debt and IVAs, which will help you navigate your way through the often bewildering jungle of jargon and terminology. Make use of it as much as you need – once you understand a few key terms, everything begins to make a lot more sense.

In the next section, I look at the pros and cons of IVAs as compared with Bankruptcy and Debt Management Plans. If you want a more in-depth comparison, I recommend *IVA, Bankruptcy and Other Debt Solutions: The Definitive Guide*, by James Falla.

The IVA vs. other debt solutions

Most of this book focuses on the IVA, as compared to Bankruptcy or a Debt Management Plan. It is perhaps the most complicated debt solution and so the one that needs the most explanation. But although having debt written off sounds great, it is important to recognise that the IVA is not for everyone. Different situations require different solutions. So, before examining the IVA in detail, it is worth comparing it with the other debt solutions out there.

Bankruptcy

This solution is appropriate if you have debts that you can't afford to repay and your liabilities are greater than your assets. If you are a homeowner, your house will be repossessed and sold for the benefit of the creditors. If you have a car worth more than £1500, this will also be repossessed. Although your Bankruptcy will normally last for only one year, your credit rating will be damaged over a period of six years and you will be required to declare it if specifically asked.

Your name will be published in your local paper and the London Gazette. During your Bankruptcy you will not be able to hold the position of Company Director. You will also be restricted from joining the police force, military, accountancy and legal professions, and many jobs that require security clearance. You will also not be allowed to use a current account, only a basic account without overdraft facilities or a cheque book.

If you are on benefits you are allowed to declare yourself bankrupt. Once you are declared bankrupt all interest is frozen, and you are completely protected from further creditor action. You would be required to make monthly payments to the court for up to three years. This monthly payment is worked out according to your budget, and can change depending on your circumstances. It is typically between 50% and 70% of your monthly disposable income. There is no minimum level of payment, and if you can't afford to make any contribution at all, none would be required; however, this is at the discretion of the Official Receiver who supervises your Bankruptcy. Apart from this monthly payment, all your debts are taken away from you and you are no longer responsible for repaying them.

You may wish to consider Bankruptcy if:

- Your disposable income is not high enough to propose an IVA
- You have no property or valuable assets to protect
- Your job will not be affected by Bankruptcy

Bankruptcy pros and cons

Pros	Cons
Responsibility for repayment of debts taken away	Credit rating damaged for six years from the start of Bankruptcy, and you are required to declare your Bankruptcy thereafter if asked
One single affordable monthly payment if you can afford it	All assets, including your house and cars worth more than £1500, would be seized
An end to your debts. Bankruptcy lasts one year, the payment plan three years	During your Bankruptcy you are subject to employment restrictions
Protection from creditor action	Taking unsecured credit is prohibited during Bankruptcy
Monthly payment is adjustable according to your circumstances	You are subject to bank account restrictions; limited to a basic account
	Your income and expenditure is reviewed annually and the payment may be raised or lowered
	Your name is published in the local paper and the London Gazette as having gone bankrupt
	Private pension contributions may need to be suspended

Debt Management Plan (DMP)

This solution may be right for you if you have debts which can be completely cleared by making reduced monthly payments in less than five years. Negotiations would be made with your creditors to agree reduced payments and frozen interest on a temporary basis. As the DMP is an informal solution, there is no obligation to release equity from your house and no disposal of assets.

The longer the DMP runs, the more your credit rating will be damaged. The fact that you are in a DMP is not made public in any way. The DMP offers no protection from creditor action; while it may bring a respite in phone calls and letters, this will only be on a temporary basis. It is not legally binding, and creditors can resume charging interest or demand higher levels of repayment at their discretion. Your monthly payment is calculated according to your budget, and can change depending on your circumstances. The DMP does not offer any write-off of debt; you need to continue to make payments until all outstanding balances are cleared.

You may wish to consider a DMP if:

- Using your disposable income, you can pay off your debts in full in less than five years
- Your creditors are willing to freeze interest and reduce payments to an affordable level

DMP pros and cons

Pros	Cons
One single reduced monthly payment which is divided amongst creditors	Credit rating damaged increasingly as the DMP progresses
No requirement to release equity from assets	No guaranteed protection from creditor action
The DMP is not legally binding, so you can back out whenever you like	No guaranteed 'light at the end of the tunnel'
Interest and charges are usually frozen for a limited period	No write-off of debt
Monthly payment is adjustable according to your circumstances	Some creditors may not agree to freeze interest, or do so only for a short time
The DMP is not made public	
No employment or bank account restrictions	

IVA

This solution is appropriate if your liabilities are greater than your assets, you have debts of over £16,500 on three or more 'lines' of credit, and you can't fully clear these debts with your disposable income in less than five years.

Although your assets are protected, homeowners are required to release as much equity as possible from their property which will be contributed towards the IVA. Your credit rating will be damaged for six years from the start of the IVA. You are able to take a mortgage while still in the IVA but you are prohibited from taking further credit. No one will be actively notified that you are in an IVA, but the information will be available to the public on the Insolvency Register. There are no employment restrictions involved in the IVA. If your sole income is derived from benefits, you will not be eligible for an IVA. Once the IVA is approved all interest is frozen and you are completely protected from further creditor action.

You may wish to consider an IVA if:

- You have assets you want to retain control over
- It will take more than five years to pay your debts through a DMP
- Your job will be affected by Bankruptcy

IVA pros and cons

Pros	Cons
Up to 70% of debt written off	Credit rating damaged for six years from the start of the IVA
One single affordable monthly payment	Equity from assets must be released and contributed to the IVA
A definite 'light at the end of the tunnel', usually after five years	The IVA is legally binding, so you can't back out without consequences
Protection from creditor action	Taking unsecured credit is prohibited during the IVA
Frozen interest and charges for the duration of the IVA	Consistent failure to honour the IVA may result in Bankruptcy
Monthly payment is adjustable according to your circumstances	Your income and expenditure is reviewed annually and the payment may be raised or lowered
You can take a mortgage while in an IVA	You are not allowed to save significantly while in an IVA
Private and discreet, the IVA is not actively made public	50% of overtime and bonuses may need to be contributed towards IVA
No employment restrictions	Windfalls may need to be contributed towards IVA
Equity release can reduce IVA term	

Chapter One:

The Debt Spiral

If you are reading this book, the chances are that you, or someone close to you, has a high level of unsecured debt and wants to do something about it. According to a recent survey, the number of people with debts of ten thousand pounds or more is a massive 81%. However, in many cases it's possible to head the problem off before a serious debt solution will be needed.

People find themselves in debt for all kinds of reasons. Sometimes, these reasons are beyond a person's control. Accidents, bereavements, illness, and depression can all be causes of debt. The topics covered in this chapter are by no means comprehensive, but are some of the most common and, most importantly, preventable causes of debt.

The temptation of easy credit

One of the main reasons for the increase in personal debt is the ease with which people have had access to credit in recent years. We live in a culture where people want everything now. On the one hand, credit adds a degree of convenience to our lives. It makes it easier to book a flight online or spread the burden of purchases over a longer period of time.

But most consumers don't take into account the true cost of borrowing when using credit. Most people only consider the level of minimum repayment, rather than the interest rates or how much they will end up paying back in total. This state of affairs is made more complex by the fact that loans, credit cards and overdrafts all work on a different set of rules.

Many people are playing with fire; credit can spiral out of control very quickly, and the consequences can be disastrous. From the creditors' point of view, this is a good thing. Although much media attention has been given to the debt mountain in the UK, the statistics work in the creditors' favour, '56% of people pay their credit card bill on time', and only around 5% of bank lending becomes bad debt'. This means that there is a group of 39% of people who don't pay their bills on time and yet don't fall into insolvency – and they are the ones who end up paying a small fortune to the creditors in interest and late payment charges. There is big money to be made in debt, and a 5% write-off of bad debt is, from the creditors' point of view, only a minor concern. This means that the banks are absolutely motivated to sell credit to as many people as they possibly can. The more credit they sell, the more money they make.

As soon as young people turn 18 in this country, they are bombarded with offers of credit. We are encouraged to look at the repayments rather than the total when considering whether or not we can afford to take the debt on. All this makes it exceptionally easy to fall into debt, and as many people are becoming aware, it can be a very slippery slope.

My story

I first opened my shop using a £14,000 lump sum of redundancy money that I had received from my old employer. At the beginning everything was going well – the shop was flourishing and making a great profit, and I didn't have a single credit card. But that didn't stop the banks from offering them to me. Every day I received several letters and leaflets through the post advertising new rates on loans and credit cards. But at the time, I just wasn't interested. I had no need to rely on credit as I was fairly comfortable.

Unfortunately, pride came before a fall. My brother was an estate agent at the time and was impressed by how well my shop was doing. He asked if he could come on board, and I accepted. We decided to expand, and bought another premises that he would be responsible for. This new purchase used up all the savings I had. The only flaw in the plan was the fact that my brother had no retail experience and didn't seem to have the same touch with the customers that I had. To cut a long story short, after six months the shop folded and we had to shut it down. The problem was that I was tied into a lease, so I ended up paying a lease on a shop that was not turning over any profit. This, combined with the flamboyant lifestyle which I had developed in parallel with the success of my first shop, meant that I began to rely heavily on credit cards and loans.

The leaflets kept coming through the door, and I began to take them up on their offers. All I had to do was fill in the forms and send them off – it was as simple as that. My collection of credit cards gradually grew. At first, the ease with which I got credit felt like an absolute blessing. I saw it as a vital lifeline, a way of keeping myself afloat, and never suspected that I would end up being unable to pay it back.

As my personal debt levels gradually rose, I realised I needed to do something to ease the financial pressure. In retrospect, what I should have done was cut back on the family spending, perhaps even downsized the house or the car, and consolidated my business activities. But at the time I was flushed from the success of my first shop, and the failure of the second shop seemed more like a glitch in an otherwise upward financial curve. Filled with optimism – and, looking back, naiveté – I mistakenly thought that the best way to improve things would be to open up another shop, this time learning from the mistakes that my brother and I had made before. To be honest, I really didn't want to suffer a downturn in our spending or lifestyle. My wife and children were very happy with the life we were leading and I didn't want to disappoint them with cutbacks. The other shop opened and I tried my best to make it work.

Meanwhile, my unsecured debt situation was worsening. The bank kindly offered to consolidate my debts with an unsecured loan, then extended my overdraft, then offered me another credit card.

They didn't seem to be concerned that I was already in a significant level of debt – they just kept offering me solutions, telling me that my credit rating was excellent. At the time I couldn't understand how it could be excellent, but I wanted the money so much that I didn't ask any questions (for more on credit ratings see the next section, 'Robbing Peter to Pay Paul'). On the business side too I was feeling the strain; the new shop was not really taking off and I found myself extending the terms from my suppliers again and again. My suppliers bent over backwards to help me get by, but in reality I don't think they had any idea of how bad things were getting.

In a misguided attempt to generate more income, I ended up opening yet another shop. I had to shell out thousands and thousands of pounds in order to pay the legal fees, and I took the shop on a five year lease. And where did the money come from? Unsecured debt. The banks were only too happy to oblige. All the time I was in severe denial, putting my head into the sand and trying to keep chipper and cheerful. If the first shop was such a success, I told myself, surely this one will be too! What I didn't take into account, of course, is that the other shop had barely any overheads; this new place came with thousands of pounds of expense before we even got started.

The ease with which I got credit was shocking. What I really should have done is sat down with a pencil and paper, and perhaps an accountant or a financial advisor, and worked out my business and personal accounts, completed a future trading projection, a profit and loss sheet, and details of my personal and business income and expenditure. But I was in such a panic at the time that I simply ran headlong into another large financial commitment, desperately trying to get myself back on track and provide for my family in the manner to which they had become accustomed. And the banks welcomed me with open arms.

Although I can't pretend that the situation was not my fault, I also believe that I was in part a victim of the creditors' lax lending practices. My advice is to look beyond the creditor's sales patter, sit down with a realistic budget sheet and work out what you can actually afford to borrow and what you can't. Then you will be in a clearer frame of mind to take appropriate action.

IVA.co.uk Forum Members' Stories

Angela Pole, Leicester

'There didn't seem to be a particular reason why my debts built up – there was no redundancy, period of illness or anything like that, although I was unemployed at one point. They just seemed to gradually accumulate and before I knew it they were unmanageable.

'At first my overdraft began to take the strain of overspending, just trying to pay the bills and feed the kids. No cars, expensive holidays, or anything like that. Then I bought a computer on hire purchase, as I had been offered a job working from home. But the offer fell through. Then we took a loan out to repay the computer loan and credit card. The bank offered the loan to me so easily – I thought that since I could get credit this easily there couldn't be that much of a problem.'

'Later on I tried to manage my debts by consolidating all the debts into one loan, but I felt too embarrassed to mention the original loan so it was left out of the consolidation. This meant that I was making two payments each month rather than one, and this was beyond my means. Things got steadily worse, and yet the banks kept offering me more credit. My overdraft grew to a level of £11,000, and at one point I had a £50,000 limit on one single credit card! It was just ridiculous. Eventually, my total debt stood at £72,000. Things simply spiralled out of control.'

IVA.co.uk Forum Experts' Advice

Melanie Giles
Melanie Giles is an independent Insolvency Practitioner and has been working in the debt solutions industry for over twenty years.

'In my experience, the main reason why people get into debt is financial naiveté, a lack of awareness to the true cost of borrowing, and, to a certain degree, irresponsible lending on the part of the banks.

Most of my clients started borrowing pretty much as soon as they left school, with a credit card linked to their first current account, often on their eighteenth birthday. This can lead to more credit being taken out on new cards, the use of store cards as a result of discounted sales offers from retailers, and later maybe a bank loan to consolidate the debts into a lower repayment. It is often a pattern for consumers to then continue to use the original sources of credit, rather than closing the accounts and getting rid of the cards. In this way, the debts grow and grow.

Credit cards are often seen as status symbols and the temptation to spend often comes from peer pressure. And of course the banks should not be offering these potentially dangerous credit facilities so freely in the first place. Credit cards work along a simple set of principles, but they are deceptively easy to acquire and easy to abuse. People don't tend to sit down and do their sums. They rarely consider what APR really means, and what they will actually end up paying back compared to the amount they borrow. The minimum repayments on credit cards are fairly low these days, which of course means that the banks have more of an opportunity to charge interest over an extended period. So people inevitably end up equating the cost of borrowing to the minimum monthly payments rather than the APR, which creates a false view of what they owe. When I sit down with my clients and work out what they owe, it can sometimes end up being twice as much as they think! It is clear that a lot of people are not used to budgeting these days.

'The problem is compounded by bad practice on the behalf of lenders, such as the advertising of credit facilities in the form of junk mail. Lenders don't appropriately check their customers' circumstances. They only have visibility of a credit rating report, which merely discloses the status of payment history on each account. But a lot of people get into the 'debt spiral', which means maintaining repayments using borrowed money. The credit report bears no indication of the total amount that is owed, let alone if someone can afford to service the repayments or not.'

Mark Allen

Mark Allen is a partner in the accountancy firm Grant Thornton, and is responsible for the National IVA Service Line. He is a chartered accountant, licensed Insolvency Practitioner and a regular panel member on the televised IVA.co.uk Debates.

'In my experience, I can say that one of the key reasons why people end up with debt problems is that borrowed money has been now far easier to obtain than twenty years ago. As a society we have now moved above the benchmark of the 140% debt-to-income ratio, which is actually higher than the USA. In such a situation it doesn't take much of a shock to people's circumstances to tip them over into a debt crisis. And it is disastrous how easy it is to get into such a position.'

'I work very closely with the Citizens' Advice Bureau, and have seen how this situation spiralled off in the early '80s. Suddenly there was a lot of money coming out of the system, and human nature dictates that people want money. So over the last two decades we have seen a cultural shift whereby taking credit has become more and more acceptable. In my parents' day, having a credit card was an embarrassment – it meant that you couldn't afford to buy things and had to suffer the shame of borrowing. Nowadays, on the other hand, my 4-year-old old picks up my plastic credit card and says, 'money, money!' And a big reason for this widespread change in attitude is the ease with which credit has been available. The consumer must be savvy enough to be aware of where the banks are coming from.'

Essential Advice

- When taking out a loan or credit card, make sure you check the details and small print so you know just how much the debt is going to cost you in the long run.
- In your monthly budget, set aside money that will be used to pay your debt. Don't just focus on paying off the minimum payments, pay back as much as you can each month.
- Be aware of the point of no return, where you can't make payments without resorting to further borrowing, well before you reach it.
- Look into useful budgeting schemes such as 'Think Banking' (thinkbanking.co.uk), which restrict the way in which you take your own money out of the bank. They provide a service where they set aside a portion of your income and ring-fence it and you can never touch that money, so you will always have enough in the account to cover your bills.
- Keep creditors informed at all times of your payment strategy, particularly if you start running into trouble. They would much rather see people trying to be honest and work out problems with them before they hear from a professional. They may be willing to freeze interest on suspend repayments for a few months if you discuss your problems with them.

'Robbing Peter to pay Paul'

Using credit to pay credit is commonly called 'robbing Peter to pay Paul'. This can mean a variety of things including:

- literally taking money off one card to pay another
- using up all your salary on your credit commitments, thereby forcing yourself to borrow more at the end of the month
- taking out unaffordable consolidation loans, remortgages and overdrafts

Sometimes, of course, debt consolidation can work, particularly when the debtor is able to release money from their house at a reasonable rate and pay off all their unsecured debt. However, there is a vast difference between sensible consolidation and taking out an *unaffordable* consolidation loan, or struggling blindly from one credit card to another just to get yourself by from month to month.

The system of credit scoring is such that is easy for people not to realise that they are taking on debt commitments that they simply can't afford. Credit scoring is not based on your income levels verses your debt levels; it is based on your record of missed payments. So even if you are unemployed, so long as you have not missed any payments – even if all your credit cards are being serviced by each other – this will not show up on your credit rating and you will be offered more and more credit. Thus it is easily possible to get into the habit of living on credit cards and sliding further and further into debt, while still keeping a good credit rating as a result of keeping up-to-date on all payments. The worst thing about it is that when the creditors put you under pressure to make payments this forces you into further borrowing. The longer this goes on for, the higher the amounts that you need to repay get, and the more you borrow. In this way the process accelerates until before you know it you are facing insolvency.

My story

My case became a classic one of robbing Peter to pay Paul. I got into a frame of mind where so long as I didn't miss a payment, things were going all right. Of course, this was deceptive; in actual fact, by focusing on keeping my payments up-to-date I was compounding the problem. I was prioritising debt repayments at the expense of living costs, and that meant that I was always forced to borrow more.

As a family, we had got into the habit of spending a lot when the shop was doing well; then we made the mistake of continuing with the same lifestyle when things were getting harder. Instead of selling up and curbing our lifestyle early on, I thought, or rather hoped I would get lucky again. I knew deep down that we had a problem, but in the end I just left it too late. It all came to a head around 2003 when finally all of my credit cards were maxed out to the limit, and nobody would offer me any more unsecured loans. I was left with no alternative – all I could do was begin eating into the equity in my house. I took a secured loan against the property at a very high interest rate, and used this lump sum to consolidate a portion of unsecured debt. I felt absolutely terrible, like a total failure.

Even though I had released money from my house, through sheer desperation I had signed up to an extortionate interest rate. This meant that the mortgage payments were extremely expensive, and once again I didn't have enough money to service my remaining unsecured debt. Each month, the only way I could keep the creditors happy was to borrow more in order to simply service the minimum payments on all the credit cards and loans. I continued to rob Peter to pay Paul for a little while longer, trying my best to keep my head above water for the good of the family. But then the credit ran out a second time, and I had nowhere left to turn.

IVA.co.uk Forum Members' Stories

Dominic Corby, London

'My debts started when I was at university. I didn't have a student loan; instead I relied on bank loans and part-time work to pay my way. When I left university in the early 1990s, I had accumulated £20,000 worth of debt. I managed to stay on top of this at first, but by the time I had found a reasonably paid job, my debts stood at over £45,000.

Most of this extra debt had been accumulated through the process of using credit to pay credit. I felt that missing a payment was the worst thing I could do; I felt as if I had entered into an agreement with the creditors and that to miss a payment would have been letting them down. So I made sure that I made every single payment, even if that meant borrowing more money to do so. Unfortunately, I wasn't aware of the damage that my finances were suffering. I found it very easy to continue getting credit, even though my wages couldn't cover both the minimum repayments and my living costs.'

IVA.co.uk Forum Experts' Advice

James Falla

James Falla is the Director of the debt help company Thomas Charles, and has advised people who have personal debt problems since 1997.

'Robbing Peter to pay Paul is a natural consequence of not saving for a rainy day. The underlying issue is people live up to and beyond their means so that they don't have any resources to fall back on. This puts them in a situation where if something goes wrong, or the unexpected occurs, it quickly forces them to turn to more credit. There are countless unexpected things that can trigger a debt problem, such as not properly planning for a baby, an unexpected period of unemployment, loss of overtime, a sudden illness, splitting with a partner, and so on. All of these things inevitably incur some expense, and they can be dealt with if people have savings to fall back on. But because people don't generally save for emergencies, they get caught out badly by unexpected costs.'

'A sudden increase in interest rates or mortgage payments can also cause problems, but in my view, that's just another symptom of not planning for the unexpected. Interest rate rises are a predictable and an unavoidable part of life; interest rates are inclined to rise from time to time, and a provision should be made for that.

Otherwise one has no option but to turn to credit more and more to cover the extra expense.'

Essential advice

- Work out a monthly budget you can realistically stick to, and ensure that you are putting money aside into savings. This will mean that you are able to survive unforeseen events without relying on credit.
- Never take money off one card in order to pay another.
- Be particularly aware if you are getting into the habit of regularly using credit cards at the end of each month. This is usually a sign that things are slipping out of control.
- When considering consolidation, take great care to think it through before signing on the dotted line. Never sign up for credit impulsively, or in the heat of the moment; only agree to a consolidation offer if you are sure that the repayments will fit within your budget.
- If you are a homeowner and thinking about consolidation, seriously consider lowering your mortgage payments by changing onto an interest-only mortgage, or one with lower rates. You can always change it back again in a few years when you are in a better position. Be wary, however, of increasing your secured lending to the extent that you put your home at risk.

Mixing personal and business debts

Self-employed people need to be particularly careful to keep a separation between their business and personal debts. It is all too easy to rush headlong into business and personal transactions without keeping proper accounts and records of what you are spending, what you are buying and for what purpose. In such a scenario it doesn't take very long before your finances are in a complete mess and you lose sight of your monthly budget. Once this has happened there is a very real danger of over-extending yourself financially, all because your income, expenditure and budgeting is in a muddle.

Another problem with relying on business-related lines of credit for personal matters and vice versa arises if you overlook the necessity of making a provision for tax. When your gross income arrives, it will feel as if all of that money belongs to you; in fact this is not the case, as around a quarter of it belongs to the taxman. Once you have become accustomed to spending your gross income, it is very easy to take credit that can only be maintained by a consistent level of income at this level. Of course, this means that in reality you are not earning enough to service your debt – what you are spending is actually the taxman's money. When April comes around you will certainly be faced with a huge tax bill which you will find difficult to pay, especially if you are pinned down by hefty credit commitments every month.

My story

When I started my business I had no prior experience in the field – my background was supermarket management, which is the type of job where you do your hours and get your pay at the end of the month. Being self-employed was a completely different ball-game. And because the supermarket made me redundant, the transition from being on the payroll to being my own boss was very sudden. Within six months, I had my own shop. Within eight months, I was trading. Surprisingly enough, within a year I was making a decent profit and in eighteen months business was booming. As it turned out, I had been in the right place at the right time; there was a real niche for a friendly local grocer who could provide a better quality and range of produce than the faceless, impersonal supermarket. I just happened to be the lucky one that got in there when the chance came up. It was like a dream come true, and lulled me into a false sense of security.

I found that being my own boss had massive advantages. Initially, I was worried that I might become lazy if I had no boss, no rules to follow or targets to hit. But in reality it was the other way round. I put everything I had into making the business a success. I would go to work smiling, and come back tired but happy. Before long we could afford to go on holiday again, and I bought myself a Mercedes as a special treat –a reward for all my hard work. Who would have thought that being made redundant could be the best thing that happened to me?

The problem was that I was so swept off my feet that I didn't give my accounts due care and attention. The effect of this was that the line between business and personal expenses was non-existent. At the time this didn't seem to matter, as there was more than enough money to go round. Indeed, I don't even think that I was aware that there was another way of doing things.

Things began to take a nosedive when my brother came on board. As a result of the early success, I had a certain aura of invincibility about me, and he was keen to join my business. We began to expand, shop by shop, but frustratingly enough none of the other shops enjoyed the good fortune of the first. Indeed, they were almost exclusively running at a loss. This was when my debts began to mount up, and the downward spiral was accelerated by the confusion in my accounts that existed up to that point. My brother was made a cardholder on my personal credit cards, as were the managers of the other two shops. The idea was that they would be able to have access to credit when dealing with suppliers, and that is exactly what they did; they are all honest people and none of them took advantage of the facility. But the effect was disastrous, as my personal debt levels escalated rapidly. At the time I felt that I would rather owe money to a bank than the suppliers, as I had forged a good relationship with many of them and I didn't want to let them down. Of course, when the commercial sources of credit began to dry up I inevitably got into debt with the suppliers as well. The mixing of business and personal debt just meant that I had landed myself in hot water on a personal level as well as in business.

Another factor that added to the general mess was the fact that when I consolidated my debts through releasing money from my house, a good portion of that money went towards propping up the business which by that point was failing anyway. That meant that my house was linked to the welfare of the business, and because there wasn't enough money in the house to consolidate both my business and personal debts, I ended up with the worst of both worlds.

IVA.co.uk Forum Experts' Advice

Melanie Giles
Melanie Giles is an independent Insolvency Practitioner and has been working in the debt solutions industry for over twenty years.

'Proper business planning is an absolute must for self-employed people if they are going to avoid falling into unmanageable debt. Since new regulatory standards came in some time ago, it has been a requirement for all self-employed people to have a face-to-face meeting with an Insolvency Practitioner before proposing an IVA – they can't just put it together over the phone as within simple consumer debt cases.'

'The result of this is that I have spent a lot of time going through accounts with self-employed people recently, and it is alarming to note the lack of understanding some traders have with regard to their business accounts and the need to set money aside for their six-monthly payments to H M Revenue & Customs. Often, it turns out that people owe twice as much as they thought they did, particularly when there is a debt to the Revenue authorities that they haven't taken into account.'

'If you are self-employed and you think that you might have a debt problem on your hands, the first thing to do is take a long, hard look at your business, get your accounts up-to-date and seek to draw a clear line between your business and personal liabilities.'

James Falla

James Falla is the Director of the debt help company Thomas Charles, and has advised people who have personal debt problems since 1997.

'It is not uncommon for business owners, either Directors of small limited companies or sole traders, to mix their personal and business liabilities by taking out personal guarantees on loans. If you are a small business owner, the number one rule is to keep your business and personal accounts very separate. If they become mixed together, for example by having only one bank account into which all income is deposited for personal as well as business usage, then that can be the start of potential issues. This is particularly the case when you don't have a sensible control over what money is coming in, what is a business expense and what is a personal expense, and what your potential tax liabilities are. Such confusion quickly spreads throughout your financial affairs, and the end result is often a debt crisis.'

Essential Advice

- Focus on the management and organisation of your finances from the beginning of your business, and ensure that business and personal income and expenditure are kept as separate as possible.
- Make sure that you have at least two bank accounts, one for your business and the other for your personal use.
- Keep a regular tax calculation on an ongoing basis, and if possible set aside a tax allowance every month into a designated account. This will ensure that you are not taken by surprise when the tax year ends.
- If you have no choice but to fund your business by taking personal debt, make sure that you have a designated credit card or loan that is only used for business expenses. This will make things far easier to understand, and you will be able to maintain a distinction between the two areas of your financial life.

Denial and fear of failure

Many people in the UK are in a position where they have been offered a great deal of credit and can now only just cover their repayments. At that point there are countless things which can push them into unmanageable debt; they can be job related, such as an income reduction, redundancy or loss of overtime. Or it may be a business venture that turned into a disaster for whatever reason. Family-related issues such as bereavement, divorce, wedding, or high levels of child maintenance can also cause problems. Or it may be down to increased rent levels, the purchase of a house, or simply overspending.

Once the debt problem has become serious, almost everybody goes through a period in which they put their heads in the sand. Admitting to yourself that you actually have a significant debt problem often amounts to the same thing as admitting failure, and many people will resist this at all costs. Unfortunately, this means the debt crisis can get quite bad before the debtor finally reaches the tipping point, realises something has to be done and asks for help. The cruel irony is that if they had asked for help earlier it would have been far easier to resolve.

This fear of admitting failure is one reason the IVA.co.uk forum can be an invaluable resource. Many people feel like they are struggling with their debt problem alone, so it can be a huge comfort to find a forum of like-minded people who have gone through similar experiences. Everyone there has either had debt crises themselves or has worked professionally with people in similar situations for many years. The IVA.co.uk forum is also completely anonymous. You can log on with a username that is not connected to your real name, and communicate for as long as you choose without revealing your identity. This can be a great help when taking the major step of seeking help, as you can feel safe in the knowledge that nothing that you say will impinge on your real-life situation and there is no threat of embarrassment or exposure.

My Story

At a certain point things began to spiral steadily downwards, and there was nothing I could do to stop it. One of the weird things about being in debt is that each time you think things can't get any worse, suddenly they do; then you find yourself wishing that things were merely as bad as they had been a few weeks before. And then things get worse again, and you wish that you could turn back the clock a couple of weeks. Then things get worse again. It is extraordinary how much fortitude you develop when this process goes on and on. It's like you go numb, or you develop a kind of split personality, so that part of you is worrying like hell about the debt while the rest of you is keeping up a cheerful front. So much of it is about maintaining your image, not letting on to people in the local pub, let alone your friends and family, that you are actually going under.

For many years, I kept my burgeoning debt issues to myself as a result of a pervasive state of denial. Deep down, I just didn't want to have to go through the humiliation of admitting defeat to myself, my wife or anyone else. As I was working for myself, I was the one making all of the decisions; our family followed the traditional model whereby I looked after the finances and Bev looked after the kids. Unfortunately, that meant that I became increasingly alienated because I never spoke to her about the extent of the problem. So far as she was concerned everything was fine, as all the evidence pointed that way; we had a big house, a nice conservatory for Sunday mornings, and I was still driving the plush Mercedes which I had bought when I first hit the jackpot with the shop. Emotionally speaking, I bottled it up.

At the time, if you would have suggested to me that I had an emotional problem resulting from an abuse of credit, I would have told you where to get off. Looking back, though, I can certainly admit that emotional issues made my debt situation a lot worse. I have never really been one for the touchy-feely side of life, so I have to admit I never seriously went into the underlying emotional issues that may have been at work in producing the mess that I ended up in.

Even though I never really got to the bottom of what was driving me towards debt, deep inside, there is one issue that I can talk about: denial. Through my time on IVA.co.uk, I've found that almost every person with a debt problem experiences denial. When I was getting into debt and it was in danger of spiraling out of control, I just didn't accept it and pushed it to the back of my mind. It is as if for some strange reason the more money you owe, the more you continue to spend. I think it is a kind of 'in for a penny, in for a pound' way of thinking. If you are spending on credit cards and feeling bad about it, but at the same time going into a state of denial, then deep down you start to feel guilty. Then you lose all your confidence and self control, and continue to burn the plastic more and more. It almost makes you feel better, in a masochistic way. Perhaps it is a form of addiction.

All I wanted to do was get things back on track, and for the problem to simply go away. It just didn't seem fair, so I developed a kind of unhealthy happy-go-lucky attitude, a sort of misplaced optimism. "Don't worry," I would reassure myself, "it will all work out in the end." Somehow you keep telling yourself to think positive, you try to persuade yourself that things will get better, even though deep down you know that they won't. It was a very a bleak time, you don't think straight when you have a lot of debt, all you can think about all day is juggling money around. You get into a very strange, warped emotional state, almost obsessive. I can remember feeling euphoric when I woke up in the morning and I had not gone over my overdraft limit! The debt takes over your life and becomes all-consuming. I kept telling myself things would get better eventually.

Two things shocked me out of this state of denial. First, one of my cheques bounced for the very first time in my life, and secondly, a short while later the Diners Club petitioned for my Bankruptcy. I felt like an abject failure. I was eaten up by embarrassment. I went within myself; I didn't want to talk to people. I began to suffer from depression and sleepless nights, and started to wonder what it would be like to be dead.

What you need to do is get to a point where you can let go of denial and instead develop a feeling of acceptance. The hardest point of acceptance is when you tell the people involved, 'I have a problem'. As you can see from many of the case studies in this book, most people with debt problems experience the same pattern – they know they have a problem, but don't do anything about it for around six months to a year. The most important advice will always be: act now. Getting into debt isn't something to be ashamed of. It's a problem like any other, and the only way to deal with it is to acknowledge it, accept it, and then try and find a solution.

IVA.co.uk Forum Members' Stories

Sara Smith, Gloucestershire

'One of the key factors in the buildup of my debt was the cost of living; I took out a mortgage on a property while I was on a fairly low salary. A few years ago everyone was able to get credit more easily and the banks were throwing mortgages at people.'

'I was so far in debt that I was using my credit cards to pay my minimum payments on other cards. I was in a terrible state and my health was affected too. I felt constantly down and was even lying to my parents and friends about my money situation.'

Stephen Parry, Wales

'Most of my debts were accumulated as a result of my wife falling sick. This meant she had to cut down the hours she worked considerably and in turn I had to in order to care for her. This was a massive change in our income. We started to take out unsecured debt to help us keep living as we were before, which mounted up and eventually became a problem.'

IVA.co.uk Forum Experts' Advice

Richard Reid

Richard Reid is the founder of the Pinnacle Therapy Wellbeing Group. He is a professionally qualified counsellor, hypno-psychotherapist and mediator.

'Fear of failure is one of the main reasons that people don't address their debt problems until they are at a crisis point. I often ask my clients, "Where is the evidence that people see you as a failure?" I encourage them to question the things that they previously took for granted and assess whether or not they are reasonable or helpful.

'Often counselling such clients involves 'holding a mirror' up to them in order to encourage them to understand more fully the destructive and ultimately futile nature of their behavior. This can often serve to provide the motivational springboard for then working with the client to promote a greater degree of self-worth.

'Another important step to take in getting out of the state of denial is to engage in self-reflection. For example, if you are buying expensive things on a regular basis, question yourself. Ask, "Do I actually need these things I am buying? Why am I compelled to buy these things?" A little emotional enquiry and reflection is a good idea – it can help to give you a degree of objectivity, and to start to recognise the problem and see the need for a solution.

'One major emotional cause of debt is low self-esteem. If people have doubts about their own character, or a general sense of inferiority, they may be compelled to compensate for their anxiety through buying things. When this happens, it is very hard for the debtor to cut back their spending. They feel compelled to maintain this standard in order to be perceived as a success, and to feel like a worthwhile human being – they have to keep up the façade, and this can be draining both emotionally and financially. A big part of keeping up the illusion that everything is fine is never missing a payment. In most cases this means taking out more and more credit.'

Melanie Giles
Melanie Giles is an independent Insolvency Practitioner and has been working in the debt solutions industry for over 20 years.

'In my experience, some issues which lead to unmanageable debt are comfort spending, emotional issues which distract you from addressing worsening finances, spending to keep partners and children happy, not owning up to debts to a partner for fear of this affecting the relationship, and the sheer embarrassment of admitting failure. I am also seeing a lot of cases where people have gambled in the belief that they can win money to address their worsening debts, but as most of us know the only real winners are the bookmakers themselves.'

'Once people acknowledge the problem and share it, often with a stranger or a qualified professional, they often feel they are on the road to recovery. Sometimes you are more likely to talk about problems to strangers – and the introduction of specialised help forums such as IVA.co.uk enable people to discuss their difficulties and seek advice on a completely anonymous basis.'

'I have found on numerous occasions that husband and wife will sometimes not sit and talk to each other about such issues because it causes rows and tension. So it can sometimes be easier to lay your cards on table with an insolvency professional. People feel the burden has been taken from their shoulders and they have passed it to someone else, and in a sense this can be a positive step.'

Essential Advice

- Bear in mind that you are not alone. Hundreds of thousands of people experience serious debt problems every year in the UK. This means that there are solutions out there.
- Use online forums, such as IVA.co.uk, to seek advice and discuss your problems anonymously.
- Find a way of relating to yourself that allows you to admit to having debt problems without feeling like a failure.
- Make sure that your partner and close family know what is going on. This can prevent feelings of isolation, and it will be far easier to move forward with a solution.
- Contact a professional early. There are plenty of reputable companies who will offer this service for free and you can move forward with a greater clarity in your finances.
- Most importantly, act as soon as possible. Things will not get better by themselves, but with action you can certainly find a solution.

Chapter Two:

Finding a solution

Obviously, in an ideal world you will manage to identify and tackle a debt problem before it gets too big to handle. But this is not always as easy as it sounds. First of all you need to admit to yourself that you need to seek help; then there is the matter of breaking the news to your friends and family. After that, how do you find a professional you can trust?

Breaking the news to friends and family

The first step to seeking help is to get the issue out in the open with those closest to you. Many of the people I have encountered through IVA.co.uk are struggling with their debt crises by themselves, having kept it secret from their nearest and dearest. This can be because of a sense of pride, an unwillingness to admit failure, or a fear that their debt problems may trigger an end to their relationship.

While these are difficult issues to resolve, it is almost always best to share the problem with your family or friends. Once you have the support from your partner, you can make the key decisions together knowing that they are behind you every step of the way, and it's a lot easier to just accept the necessary change in circumstances and look towards the future.

My story

Once I finally recognized that my debts had got the better of me, I felt completely defeated. Although my wife knew there was something going on, she had no idea about the true extent of the problem. I had got to the point where I didn't want to open the post, and because I didn't want my wife to come across the letters, this big pile of red letters accumulated in the bottom drawer of my desk. I was in the habit of secretly checking my bank balance first thing every morning to see how far I was from my overdraft limit – if I had anything available at all, perversely enough things didn't feel so bad. Later on, once I had come to my senses, I thought, "It doesn't matter what my wife thinks of me. I have to be honest. Let's just get this debt thing sorted and get on with our lives." And that was when I really began to turn things around.

I finally plucked up the courage and talked things through with my wife. For a long time I found the prospect of telling Bev absolutely terrifying. Although I knew that in the end she would need to be told, I was worried about how she would react.

It was one of the most painful conversations with Beverly that I have ever had in my life, and it is a conversation that I never want to have again. In the long run, though, I think that sharing the experience with her was a key factor in finding a solution. Although my wife was upset, and understandably so, it really helped that she was so supportive. We both absolutely agreed that we had to take the bull by the horns and get things sorted. Once we had agreed on what we were going to do, it wasn't so bad – we resigned ourselves to it. Before long, the whole village knew what was happening. But once we got over everyone knowing, and accepted it, it wasn't that hard after all.

In reality, I didn't have too many friends at that point anyway; at the time I was working all the hours that God sent and I had been doing so for a while. It wasn't me I was worried about, it was Bev. She had a lot of friends, and to tell them that we had fallen off the perch was very difficult. Especially living in a village, as we do, everyone knows everyone else's business and has a good old chinwag about it in the local pub.

Having told my wife, I then had to break the news to my family. I remember we had a big family meeting about it; I think it was my sister's idea. I felt like I was being tried by a judge and a jury! As it turned out, my family was split down the middle. Half of them felt I had wasted the money, whereas the other half were sympathetic. Although I didn't admit to it at the time, looking back I can see with the benefit of hindsight that in a way I had lost the money through making some bad business decisions. My mother didn't understand that, though; she has never had much of a head for business. She was convinced that I had gone out spending willy nilly, and she gave me what for, I can tell you. My dad just could not understand the situation at all. He kept saying, "But why are you putting your kids through this? Why are you putting your kids through this?" that hurt a lot at the time.

I think by that stage I felt so low about myself that however bad their opinions of me were, they were never going to be as bad as the opinion that I held of myself. So to a certain extent I was immune to their criticisms, or at least I thought I was at the time. It was as if I was holding the world at a distance, and I just had no idea why I was feeling the way I was feeling.

The problem is that people can't empathize with you unless they have been in the same situation themselves. There is just no way they can fully understand what it is really like to be in that level of debt, and how it is so easily done. They think you are some sort of spending machine, when in actual fact the opposite is probably the case; for me, at least, it was simply a matter of a horrible chain of events leading one thing to another. But it is difficult for family to understand the ins and outs of this, especially when they are all together in the same room and emotions are high and everyone is shouting over everyone else.

My family didn't know the whole story because I didn't tell them about the full extent of the debt. But a few days after the meeting they all helped out financially, they all chipped in. Then I realized that I wasn't alone in the world, that my family really did care about me. The money that they offered me was nowhere near enough to get me out of the hole, but it made life more bearable in the short term. I was in a depression, it was a very bleak time, and the support of my family was essential.

IVA.co.uk Forum Members' Stories

Angela Pole, Leicester

'I wanted to have a prospective solution on the table before I broke the news to my friends and family. I wanted to show that there was a way out and that I had taken steps to remedy the situation already. At that stage my family had not even heard of an IVA, and knew nothing about it. Nevertheless, it really helped to finally speak to people about the problem and not keep it all inside.'

IVA.co.uk Forum Experts' Advice

Melanie Giles

Melanie Giles is an independent Insolvency Practitioner and has been working in the debt solutions industry for over twenty years.

'Friends and family can be enormously supportive. Professionals look for the technical and commercial solution, and probably lose sight of the need for emotional support. That's where friends and family, especially partners, are important. Most importantly of all, you must recognize you have a problem as soon as possible, and understand that further borrowing will not help.'

Richard Reid

Richard Reid is the founder of the Pinnacle Therapy Wellbeing Group. He is a professionally qualified counselor, hypno-psychotherapist and mediator.

'Everyone has things in their heads called 'injunctions', which are unwritten rules that we live by. Sometimes they work for us, but sometimes we work for the rules. It is easy to become slaves to the rules we have in our lives, and this can make people feel forced to continue spending and keep the situation under wraps. So part of the healing process is about questioning those and challenging them.'

'One recent case of mine springs to mind. I had a client who had been made redundant. His debt was spiraling out of control. When we actually started to talk, one of the reasons things were so difficult was his sense of pride. He was unwilling to talk about his problem, and this made him snappy with his family. His relationship became strained, he got moody, his health suffered, his life was a mess. The reason for this was the simple injunction, "I am not allowed to show weakness". He wanted to feel like the provider. We spoke about it, and it emerged that deep down he was frightened. He hadn't applied for a job since leaving school, and this situation was a new and terrifying one for him. So we looked at ways to overcome the fear and broach the subject with his brother and parents. The simple act of telling them helped, and he found that they could lend him some money too.'

'As the old adage goes, 'a problem shared is a problem halved'. Even if a friend or relative is unable to provide practical assistance in dealing with debt issues, often simply providing a sympathetic ear can be enough.'

Essential advice

- Don't feel that you are obliged to deal with the situation all by yourself. Whatever solution you decide to take, the support of friends and family is going to be vital.
- Remember that people may be hurt if you have been hiding your problems, but that they will want to help you to find a solution.
- If you feel unable to confide in your friends and family, find a professional advisor who you can share your problem with. It may be easier to talk to family members if you can discuss the debt solution you are going to use with them.
- Try to be totally honest. Playing down the level of debt or concealing certain problems won't help matters. It is best to come clean.

Finding help

As soon as you begin to look at debt solutions, you will be overwhelmed by the sheer amount of companies offering their services, each claiming that their particular method is the best. All you need to do is type 'IVA' or 'debt advisor' into an Internet search engine to see that the amount of companies out there is phenomenal. The problem is that not all of these companies are good, and not all have the interests of the consumer at heart. The last thing you want is to be saddled with an arrangement that is not to your best advantage just because such-and-such a company wants to make money out of you. Having said that, there are some very reliable and reputable companies out there who charge little or no fees and provide very good advice. The important question is: how do I choose the right company for me?

My story

When I made my first attempt to get professional help, I had been leafing absentmindedly through the local paper one morning when I came across an advert for a debt solutions company. Without doing any research at all I got in touch with them by phone, and was put through to a girl in a call centre who asked me lots of details about my debts, my employment, my family, and my income and expenditure. At the end of the conversation she told me that she would "post me out some forms". I said that I looked forward to receiving them, but I hadn't a clue what the forms were for. True to her word, the forms arrived the next day. I opened the letter, took one look at the twenty-page document that I was supposed to sit down and fill out, and stuck it back in the envelope again. I just couldn't face the hassle of all this form-filling, and I had no idea what function the form served anyway.

I put the issue to the back of my mind again for another few weeks, and then I sought professional help once again. This time I was more successful. I contacted an Insolvency Practitioner in my area that I had found in the phone book – once again I did no further research – and arranged to go in for a meeting the following week. In the end the meeting was successful and I ended up in an IVA. But the company I used was not the best, and I had plenty of problems along the way. It is always better to research a few companies well and get their advice before committing yourself to any one person – plenty of my problems could have been avoided if I had done my research more thoroughly.

Over the last few years that I have been involved with IVA.co.uk I have seen a massive increase in debt solution companies. Most of them provide good service, but others are just out to make a quick buck. This has made me more and more convinced of the need to do careful research before committing yourself.

Online is the best place to start your research. The IVA.co.uk forums are filled with people who have gone through IVAs with many different companies, good and bad, and will be able to provide advice on choosing a good provider. At IVA.com, there are reviews and comments on numerous IVA companies. Both of these sites are useful for checking out companies that you have spoken to and are thinking about contacting.

You need to take careful advice and make sure that you fully understand what the solutions are; you must not just take someone's word for it. Understand what options are available to you; there should be about two or three, and you should be able to list the pros and cons for each. Look back at the section on page 19 and think about which solution is most appropriate for your situation.

When choosing an IVA provider, think about the kind of service that you'd like to receive. Larger companies are more established and potentially more reliable, but will inevitably provide you with less in the way of personal contact. It can be frustrating if every time you call up you have to deal with a different person who knows nothing about your case. A smaller operation can provide you with more personalised service, but you may struggle to find a reputable small operator who is close at hand. It just comes down to the kind of relationship you want with an Insolvency Practitioner, and which company you feel most comfortable dealing with.

One thing you must be careful to avoid is the quick fixes, tempting as it may appear at first. Avoid anybody who suggests your problem can be sorted very quickly and easily, or someone who is pushy and one-sided, in a word, salesmen. If you get the feeling that you are being sold to rather than advised, in my opinion the best thing to do is run a mile. Some IVA firms are getting a very bad reputation these days because they are too pushy, and I think this is justified. In addition to that, in my view you really need to be careful about consolidation loans, either from unsecured debt providers or big commercial secured loan companies. The reason for this is that consolidating your debt inevitably makes it bigger, and if the repayments are stretching you to the limit in a financial sense, you are certain to turn to other forms of credit sooner or later to plug the gaps, and the whole thing will have made matters worse rather than better. If you do consolidate, the best thing you can do is cut up your cards and avoid taking any further credit.

Some dodgy companies will take money off you, but then don't forward it to your creditors. Everything you pay goes on fees and costs, and you are even worse off than before. There are lots of these kinds of scams out there, and you should be particularly wary if you are a homeowner. There are plenty of unscrupulous companies that will provide you with a temporary solution in order to get at the equity in your house.

The most important thing to remember is that there is no reason to rush. Rushing into a debt solution is always the biggest mistake. I always say to people on the forum, "You don't have to make a decision today." Have a think about it over the weekend, discuss it with your partner or family, and then go back to your advisor when you have made a decision that you are absolutely sure about and happy with. If at any point you feel uncomfortable with the company you are dealing with, remember that there are plenty of others out there. In this way you can ensure that you are in the best possible hands.

Jonathan Tinsley, South Yorkshire

'When I started looking into debt solutions I gained some basic familiarity with the various options out there by scouring the Internet for information. I narrowed down my options to an IVA and a Debt Management Plan. Of those two I favoured the IVA, as I was put off by the length of time that a DMP would take to pay my debts. After doing some research on the Internet, I contacted a company who eventually processed my IVA.'

'The debt advisor that I spoke to initially gave me all the information and advice I needed. I was surprised at just how many variables there were, and they proved to be a good company, explaining things fully and clearly. Although my family was skeptical of the IVA – they thought that I would be better off going bankrupt – I didn't want to jeopardise a future mortgage application by going bankrupt. Eventually I decided to go for an IVA, and they supported my choice.'

IVA.co.uk Forum Experts' Advice

Mark Allen

Mark Allen is a partner in the accountancy firm Grant Thornton. He is a chartered accountant and Insolvency Practitioner with extensive experience of assisting individuals in financial difficulty.

'There are certain pitfalls to be avoided when researching debt solutions. You hear horror stories out there; it might be that only one in twenty cases goes wrong, but that is still a worrying enough percentage. I would always urge caution.'

'If you have debt problems, the last thing you want to do is pay for advice so avoid companies who want to take money off you. Most large IVA firms don't charge upfront fees, so the best thing would be to go with them. My experience of advising people who are in debt has shown me that they can often be very vulnerable on the phone. Sometimes they put total reliance and faith in you, even though they don't know you from Adam. I think if I was a rogue I could ask them for their first born son and they would consider it! If I said to half my clients, "Give me £1000 before I can help you," they would probably do it. I'm sure they would rob Peter to pay Paul to do it, but most of them would do it. Of course, if you are honourable and work for a reputable, responsible firm, that is all well and good. Otherwise that kind of blind faith can be very dangerous.'

Melanie Giles

Melanie Giles is an independent licensed Insolvency Practitioner and has been working in the debt solutions industry for over 20 years.

'The first piece of advice I would offer anybody thinking about debt solutions is before you do anything else, undertake your own research – the Internet is a great source of information, and you will often see personal recommendations for Insolvency Practitioners and debt counseling companies.'

'Check the reviews of any companies that appear to be doing a good job, and also see if you can get some informal, word of mouth views from people who have actually had the experience of dealing with particular companies or Insolvency Practitioners directly. Make sure that you take second and even third opinions, and also conduct your own research on debt forums, which provide a wealth of information from people in the same position.'

'The advantage of these resources is that they are absolutely free and open to anybody to glean information or contribute, so you can keep away from any one-sided views and opinions that you sometimes come across when dealing with companies who may have a vested interest in steering you down one course or another.'

'In general terms, I think it is best to avoid people who suggest that you borrow more in the hope the problem will go away, unless their argument is very strong and you have considered all the other options thoroughly. It is also good to avoid people who charge large upfront fees, unless there is a guarantee that you will have your money refunded in the event that the solution you wish to pursue is not accepted. Moreover, if anybody leads you to believe that the upfront fees you will be paying are going to be contributed to your creditors, they are probably not telling the truth. You must bear in mind that all commercial IVA providers make their money somehow, and it is a good idea to gain an understanding of where their money comes from before you sign up, so that you can be sure that you are going into the arrangement with your eyes wide open.'

'By the same token, be especially sensitive to people who attempt to direct you towards one particular solution rather than laying out all the options and allowing you to make your mind up for yourself. More often than not, these people have a hidden interest in you following their recommended solution, and this may not always be in your (or your creditors') best interest. Overall, there is a lot of information out there, and a number of very good companies who provide very reasonable services and sound professional advice. Take your time and, when you feel fully informed and ready to take the first step, choose what you see as being the most appropriate way forward for your future.'

Essential advice

- Contact your local Citizens Advice Bureau. All their advice is free and impartial, and they will be able to lay out the options for you.
- Carry out thorough research on the Internet. IVA.co.uk, IVA.com and similar sites can provide reviews and comments concerning most IVA companies.
- Be wary of companies who charge large up-front fees. There are plenty of places that don't charge for advice. If you decide to go with an IVA company that charges upfront fees, make sure you see in writing that the fees will be returned to you if your application for an IVA fails.
- Make sure that you understand all the options that are available to you, and the pros and cons of each. The main ones to consider are debt consolidation, a Debt Management Plan, an IVA or Bankruptcy.
- Talk to at least two or three companies before you decide which one to go with. Be sensitive to 'sales patter', and people who are pushing one particular solution.
- Take your time, and make sure you are comfortable with the company and solution you have chosen before you go ahead.

Contacting a professional

When the time comes to actually speak to a professional, be it a debt advisor or an Insolvency Practitioner, there are various pitfalls to be avoided. First of all, it is important to understand which information will be necessary to have to hand, in order to avoid having to stall or reschedule the meeting. Secondly, you must be very clear about what you can and can't afford over a five year period. If you are not vigilant with regard to your monthly budget and proposed payments, you could find yourself signing up to an unrealistic IVA proposal. This, in the long term, will mean that you may experience an unsustainable level of financial hardship.

If you have all your information clearly arranged and to hand before getting in touch with a professional, this will make your meeting far easier and more successful, and will allow you to avoid the stress and embarrassment of having to search through mountains of random paperwork to come up with the figures required.

Useful information includes:

- A detailed list of monthly household expenditure. This includes rent, mortgage payments, food, transport costs, utility bills, council tax, and any other regular expenses.

- Details of the household income including net wages (after tax), child benefits, tax credits and so on.

- A complete list of overdrafts, current store card and credit card balances, catalogue debts, unpaid bills and outstanding loans, including the start date, end date, interest rate and monthly payment of loans. Make sure you include any significant debts to friends and family as well.

- A record of any valuable assets, particularly property, including the house value, outstanding mortgage, other outstanding secured borrowing, monthly payment levels, interest rates and penalty charges

- Details of your business accounts if you are self-employed

If this list seems daunting, don't worry; a debt advisor or Insolvency Practitioner will be able to help you put it together. Do as much as you can before the first meeting, and ask for help where you need it. The more information you can provide, the quicker they can help you.

My Story

When the time came to meet with the Insolvency Practitioner, I was absolutely terrified. I put on the smartest suit I owned and headed down to London with Bev to meet the Insolvency Practitioner face-to-face. She looked very much like she knew what she was doing. After a brief exchange of pleasantries we got down to business; the ensuing conversation lasted over an hour.

As the conversation progressed, it became apparent that my personal accounts were in an absolute mess. They were all mixed up with the business debt that I had previously accrued, and in terms of tax, income and expenditure everything was in a state of chaos – not to mention all the debts that I had been juggling. I had been robbing Peter to pay Paul so much that I had almost completely lost track of where I was with everything. I couldn't remember all of the debts that I had, and the ones that I could remember I had no idea what the current balances were because I had fallen into the habit of not opening the post each day, but just putting it off and putting it off and hoping that the whole thing would just go away by itself. In the end, we had to go online and get a copy of my credit file so that we could get a list of all the debts that I had in my name. I remember that I even had to call round some of my creditors to ascertain exactly how much I owed them.

All the way through the meeting I felt like I was wearing blinkers; I didn't want to ask any questions in case it would cause her to refuse to take on my case, and as a result I ended up not really knowing what I was letting myself in for. The Insolvency Practitioner explained things very clearly and simply, but although I was nodding and smiling, deep down I wasn't really taking much of it in. I was just so desperate that she agreed to help that I would have just nodded and smiled whatever she said, really.

After the meeting, when we had gone home and fed the kids and watched a bit of telly and we were lying in bed, I felt a certain peace of mind – the first in a long, long time. Actually I didn't really understand what I was feeling until I realized that I was feeling relaxed! It was such an alien sensation. I think that deep down I realized that there was finally some light at the end of the tunnel.

It was only later on, when my IVA was approved and I had to live according to the budget that I had agreed that day in the hotel bar; that I realized I had made a mistake. I had been so keen to get the IVA approved that I had agreed to make whatever cuts in my spending was necessary to afford the IVA. And the Insolvency Practitioner allowed me to make these unmanageable cutbacks without blinking an eyelid. This was the root of my personal IVA troubles.

There were many good points about the Insolvency Practitioner as well. Most importantly, she offered us a face-to-face meeting, and took the time out to meet us and talk through our options thoroughly. I would always advise you to try and have a face-to-face meeting with an Insolvency Practitioner. The fact that they are prepared to meet you means, on one level, that they are taking it seriously – as seriously as it should be taken considering it profoundly affects your life for at least five years, and in a certain sense for much longer than that as well.

From my experience on the IVA.co.uk community forum I have learnt that people often don't get to meet the Insolvency Practitioner at all, they just deal with their staff. I personally don't think this is a good idea because the Insolvency Practitioner is the person who really has the specialist knowledge necessary for putting the IVA together. The fact is, as a debtor you inevitably feel a little foolish and humiliated, and that can act as a motivator for keeping all the professionals involved at arm's length, at the end of a phone, email, letter or whatever. But it is always worthwhile to push through that instinct, to bite the bullet and meet your Insolvency Practitioner so that you can really thrash things out properly. There are few decisions that you will take in your life that are of a similar magnitude to this one, and it is not something you should take lightly – it is not something you should rush into just on the basis of a few phone calls or letters.

But a face-to-face meeting is no good unless you are willing to ask questions and to stand your ground. When meeting with an Insolvency Practitioner, make sure that you don't just nod along and agree with whatever they say. Use it as a chance to find out what you need to know; both about the IVA process and about the relationship you will have with the Insolvency Practitioner for the next five years. What happens if there is a change in your circumstances or an unexpected cost? What happens if you miss a payment? How easy will it be to speak to the Insolvency Practitioner in person? You should get all the information you need to be comfortable before you agree to anything.

IVA.co.uk Forum Members' Stories

Angela Pole, Leicester

'The first person that I spoke to was a Debt Advisor who recommended that I apply for an IVA. The problem was that I had become dependent on my credit cards, both financially and emotionally. So when the Debt Advisor told me that I couldn't have any more credit if I went into an IVA, I couldn't go along with it. The Debt Advisor responded by saying that I 'wasn't hurting enough', and at the time I felt that he was being awfully rude. Later on, however, when things got even worse, I looked back and thought he was right. And I wished I had been hurting enough to have cut up my credit cards and proposed an IVA the first time round.'

'Either way, the second time I decided to seek help from the Citizen's Advice Bureau. By this time I was prepared to do whatever it took to get my problem solved, including getting rid of all my credit cards. At the time I had absolutely no knowledge of debt solutions, and I hoped that I would be able to come to an arrangement whereby my creditors would be happy with a small amount each week. Unfortunately my debt had grown too big for that, and I had to consider either an IVA or Bankruptcy.'

'The CAB referred me to a firm of Insolvency Practitioners. I had to go through all my details again with a Debt Advisor, and then I was passed over to the Insolvency Practitioner. I felt very confused, and didn't know who to trust; but I was in such a difficult situation that I had no choice but to proceed with the meeting. The Insolvency Practitioner helped make the decision to opt for an IVA, as the only other option was Bankruptcy. The idea of Bankruptcy scared me as I didn't want to lose my house.'

IVA.co.uk Forum Experts' Advice

Melanie Giles

Melanie Giles is an independent Insolvency Practitioner and has been working in the debt solutions industry for over twenty years.

'The ideal relationship between the client and the Insolvency Practitioner is one of complete openness, honesty and trust. I once had a client who failed to disclose fourteen thousand pounds of debt on her original IVA proposal because she knew there was a 25% minimum dividend, and also knew that if she disclosed this she wouldn't be able to raise enough funds. So she cunningly worked out how many debts to declare and kept fourteen thousand secret! Of course, two years later she paid for her folly when she realized she couldn't afford to service the remaining debt. The IVA was failed immediately, and the client was made bankrupt with a Bankruptcy restriction order for five years (usually it only lasts for one year) and a 250 hour community service order on her record as well. As Insolvency Practitioners we rely on the integrity of the client, and the majority are open and honest. Usually when they are staring you in the face, having recognized they need help, you can form a bond of trust.'

'The best advice I can give for people who are about to meet their Insolvency Practitioner for the first time is not to be afraid. Insolvency Practitioners are not there to judge you but to offer solutions to your difficulties. They are human beings with families of their own and have probably had one or two debt problems over the years themselves! The main thing to remember is that help is always out there – you just need to look for it.'

James Falla

James Falla is the Director of the debt help company Thomas Charles and has advised people who have personal debt problems since 1997.

You need to choose an Insolvency Practitioner who you have access to and feel comfortable with. They shouldn't be just a call centre. You should have access to them if you need them – that is absolutely vital. They need to be somebody you can build a relationship with.'

'If you're about to meet an Insolvency Practitioner, be prepared and organized. Write down your income and expenditure, and know why you have written what you have written. Look at your circumstances with a clear head. If you are self-employed, prepare a cash flow, and understand the difference between business and personal income and expenditure. If your partner understands the finances and household affairs but you don't, take them with you! There's no point in saying, "I don't really know because my wife deals with that."'

'In meeting the Insolvency Practitioner you should expect somebody who is an honest broker between you and your creditors – not someone who will wrap you up in cotton wool and try and get the best deal for you at the creditors' expense. The Insolvency Practitioner is a mediator between the two parties, and as such the client will be dealt with fairly but not mollycoddled. Some people expect the Insolvency Practitioner to say, "It's not really your fault and the banks shouldn't have lent money to you, it's all down to those evil banks". But what you will find is that most Insolvency Practitioners won't blame one side or the other but look at the most sensible and fair solution between the two parties.'

Essential advice

- Make sure it is possible to have a face-to-face meeting with your Insolvency Practitioner.
- Ensure that all your essential documents and accounts are organised well before the meeting, that you have a clear household budget drawn up and an approximate idea of your disposable income.
- Disclose every detail of your financial and personal affairs honestly and openly. Hiding anything at this stage can cause serious problems later on.
- Draw up a list of questions that you feel you need answers to, and make sure the Insolvency Practitioner takes the time to talk the answers through with you.
- If you feel uncomfortable for any reason, take a step back and look at other Insolvency Practitioners and the service they provide.

Andy Davie with his wife, Beverley, outside Andy's fruit and veg shop in Gamlingay, Bedfordshire

Andy Davie serves a customer at his fruit and veg shop in Gamlingay, Bedfordshire in August 2007

Andy Davie on the panel of the IVA.co.uk
Debt Debate on the Credit Crisis May 2007

Dr Vincent Cable on the panel of the IVA.co.uk
Debt Debate on Credit Culture August 2007

Audience put questions to the panel at the IVA.co.uk Debt Debate on Debt Education in October 2007

Andy Davie introduces the IVA.co.uk Debt Debate on Credit Culture August 2007

James Bellini chairs the IVA.co.uk Debt Debate on debt solutions mis-selling in February 2008

Stuart Hopewell, Melanie Giles, Mark Allen and Gill Hankey at the IVA.co.uk Debt Debate May 2008

Julian Donnelly speaks at the IVA.co.uk Debt Debate on Bankruptcy v. IVAs in May 2008

Peter Hobday fields questions at the IVA.co.uk Debt Debate on Bankruptcy v. IVAs in May 2008

Andy Reeve, Anne Kiem, James Falla, Rachel Lacey and Mark Allen debate Debt Education in Oct 2007

Chapter Three:

Submitting an IVA proposal

If you have decided upon an IVA as the solution for your debt problem, your Insolvency Practitioner will help you put together a proposal to be submitted to your creditors, who will vote on whether or not to approve it. When the time has come for this process, the temptation is to sit back and let the professionals take over. However, it is important that you keep yourself fully informed at all stages along the way – at the end of the day, it is your life that is being negotiated.

Making a good IVA proposal

It is easier than you might think to sign up to an IVA that is unrealistic and unsustainable. When people go to a meeting with an Insolvency Practitioner or speak with them over the phone, they usually have the mentality that the IVA is their only hope, without which they are doomed. This makes them desperate to get the IVA accepted. The effect of this is that they will do absolutely anything to make the IVA work – this might sound like a good thing, but in reality it can be very dangerous.

Problems arise when the IVA requires more of a financial commitment than your budget can sustain. If you agree to unrealistic cutbacks in your budget and your IVA is agreed on that basis, you have condemned yourself to up to five years of abject poverty. Under such circumstances an IVA will usually fail within a couple of years, because the pressure will get too much – an unexpected cost will push an already overstretched budget to breaking point.

An important part of making a realistic proposal is to fully understand the impact it will have on you and your finances. You should ensure that you are aware of the 'small print' on your IVA proposal. There are various clauses that may end up having a big impact on your IVA experience and personal life which are very easy to overlook. These include:

Overtime clause

This refers to a clause which is often included in an IVA under which (typically) 50% of overtime, pay rises and bonuses may be contributed towards the IVA. Many people forget about this clause when planning or signing up to an IVA, and later feel cheated when half of their overtime is taken away.

Windfall clause

Under the terms of this clause any windfall which you may receive during the IVA period, such as an inheritance, may be taken entirely and put towards paying the IVA.

Equity clause

This means that if you are a homeowner, you should fully expect to finish your IVA with no available equity in your property; this will have been contributed towards your IVA via a remortgage in the fourth or final year. This can be a critical factor in an IVA – refer to the section 'Remortgaging and Equity Release' on page 118 if you are a homeowner.

Because of the potential consequences of these clauses, it is vital to appreciate the way in which they will affect your IVA. Make sure that you bear all this in mind, and discuss them in detail with your Insolvency Practitioner in advance.

A good IVA budget will be tight but realistic. It will vary from person to person depending on circumstance, but I have included a table of expenses on the next page that shows roughly the kind of budget that is expected in an IVA. I have not included individual bills and expenses such as gas, electricity, petrol, car insurance and council tax, as these expenses are simply taken as whatever you actually pay. All figures are monthly.

	Single Debtor	Couple	Family with one child	Family with two children
Shopping	£180 - £200	£230 - £300	£330 - £400	£400 - £500
Rent / Mortgage	Below 40% of income	Below 40% of income	Below 40% of income	Below 40% of income
Mobile phone	£30	£50	£50	£50
House insurance	£25	£25	£25	£25
Car maintenance (one car)	£30	£30	£30	£30
Clothing	£20	£30	£40	£50
Contingency	£50	£50	£50	£50
Land Line	£20	£20	£25	£25

So long as you budget realistically, and are fully aware of the 'small print' clauses in your IVA, you will be putting forward a good offer to your creditors and a stable budget for yourself. If your proposal is based on faulty figures, or if you are surprised by an aspect of your IVA a few months in, the IVA is likely to fail.

My story

The Insolvency Practitioner had requested that Beverly and I meet her in the lounge bar of a big hotel in London, so I took a day off work, we made arrangements for my brother to look after the kids, we got on the train and off we went.

First, we had to go through all the details of my debts, including balances, minimum payments and so on. This was no mean feat, as my financial affairs were in total disarray. In the end we managed to clarify my entire debt situation, including all the interest. It was far worse that we had initially thought.

The next stage, after a short break, was to go through our income and expenses. Luckily amongst the paperwork in the box-file happened to be a whole sheaf of bank statements, and this was very useful in ascertaining my exact income at that time. I was extremely surprised to see how much we were actually spending each month. The Insolvency Practitioner put down allowances for clothes, food and so forth, but also the little things you forget about, like the TV license. I was amazed to see how it all added up. By the end, it was clear that we only had £250 left spare at the end of the month, which the Insolvency Practitioner referred to as our 'disposable income'. I was stunned – for the last few years we had been paying over £1000 per month to our creditors! Where on earth had that money been coming from? And then it dawned on me. The Insolvency Practitioner gave me a wry smile. "Robbing Peter to pay Paul?" she said. No wonder we were in such a mess.

The Insolvency Practitioner told us that £250 was not nearly enough money to propose an IVA on our level of debt. In order for an IVA to be successful at that time, we needed to offer the creditors at least 25p in the pound – that's 25% of the total debt, in addition to covering the fees charged by the Insolvency Practitioner. In order to afford that we would need to stump up £450 per month, and that was £200 more than we could reasonably afford, according to our initial calculations. I really felt as if I had my back against the wall, and Beverly was clutching my arm tighter than ever. It felt like she was hanging on to me for support – and it was as if all our kids were hanging off her as well.

Deep down, I had only one thought, "we need to get accepted". I didn't really know much about IVAs at the time. I had no idea, for example, that the Insolvency Practitioner drafts the proposal and then it is the creditors that choose whether or not to accept it. I thought that it would be accepted or rejected right then and there. Even when she explained the procedure to me, I was still extremely concerned that she'd agree to take the case on and propose the IVA.

It felt like my worst nightmare was coming true – she would refuse to take on our case and we would be back to square one with all of our creditors, and the next stop would certainly be Bankruptcy.

"I will do whatever it takes to make this work," I said. "I'm sure we could afford £450 per month, easy. Let's just slim down the housekeeping allowance, and take a bit off the clothing. And do we really spend that much on petrol?" The Insolvency Practitioner thought it was a fantastic idea to shed some of the expenditure to make the IVA work, and so that is what we did.

An hour later we left the hotel walking on air. The Insolvency Practitioner was going to take our case on. To this day, I remember the overwhelming sense of relief that we both felt. Beverly finally let go of my arm and started to smile again. Then we returned home, and I got the first good night's sleep I'd had in ages.

Of course it was great to have the IVA going ahead. But the harsh reality was this: we could not afford it. We simply could not afford to pay £450 per month. The problem was that I was just so desperate to get the IVA through that I would have hit myself over the head with a hammer if that would have helped. Because we were used to paying over £1000 per month to our creditors, £450 seemed relatively cheap. But the truth was that we could only comfortably afford £250, and £450 was always going to be a real stretch. When you are heavily in debt you think you will be able to scrimp and save and eat nothing but beans on toast for years. But in real life, you may be able to save like that for a month or two, but not for sixty months!

At the end of the day, I signed up for the IVA and I agreed to the budget that I put forward, and it was my responsibility to make sure the figures were realistic. Even so, I think the Insolvency

Practitioner should have warned us against making such ambitious and dramatic cutbacks.

When I assured her that we could in fact make those payments, she believed me because she wanted to believe me. I don't think it was a cynical move on her part – perhaps she wanted the business as much as I wanted the IVA, and between the two of us we ended up coming to an arrangement that simply was not realistic. At the time I didn't think that, though, I was just overcome by this profound feeling of relief, and Bev felt the same. The Insolvency Practitioner was charging no upfront fees, and she seemed very professional, so at the end of the day we had no second thoughts about it.

Nevertheless, before finally signing on the dotted line and putting the wheels in motion, we discussed it with my father-in-law but nobody else. My father-in-law had always been very much there for us. He knew we had to do something, and had always helped us out financially, so he knew the general state of our finances and appreciated how serious things had become. He was really the only person we could confide in, because people didn't really understand what IVAs were about back then. I am glad that we confided in him, even though he failed to pick up the fact that the IVA payments that I had worked out with the Insolvency Practitioner were set to squeeze our finances to breaking point and beyond.

It is not about getting the IVA accepted; it is about getting it concluded. In contrast to this, sometimes an Insolvency Practitioner tends to focused in precisely the opposite way round, wanting to tie you into the IVA as a matter of priority and then not putting so much effort in from then onwards. Therefore you must fully understand and appreciate that although it is very easy to look at your expenditure and slim it down, putting down unrealistic figures in order to make it attractive, if it won't work for five years that's absolutely no good at all – in fact, it makes matters a hell of a lot worse. Be sure that you go into the deal with your eyes open, appreciating from the start that in all probability your IVA company and your Insolvency Practitioner will all too often be focused on getting the IVA accepted.

Without being able to turn to my father-in-law for cash here and there, we would never have survived even the three years that we managed, let alone the full five years. So what I am trying to say is, an IVA can be a fantastic solution, but only if you can genuinely afford it. And I mean genuinely, without making unrealistic cuts to your budget.

In summary, then, the key advice is get your expenditure right at the beginning, and not to rush things. What happens at the beginning of the process affects the next five years, and inevitably the rest of your life.

IVA.co.uk Forum Members' Stories

Stephen Parry, Wales

'I started my IVA in 2000. There were few practitioners focusing on IVAs at the time and a friend had told me to look through the Internet. This is where I came across my IP who came to my house in Wales to discuss all of the debt solution with my wife and I. We looked at all of the areas of debt management and decided at the end of the day that an IVA would be the best option. She was completely non-judgmental throughout the whole process and explained everything clearly to me, which is how she remained throughout the entire IVA.'

'During the IVA I was also burgled which was a very upsetting experience. Our IP helped us by adding three months to end of the IVA as I had to find money to buy a new computer that I needed for work. This was a great help.'

IVA.co.uk Forum Experts' Advice

James Falla
James Falla is the Director of the debt help company Thomas Charles, and has advised people who have personal debt problems since 1997.

'Debt problems tend to put an enormous pressure on people. They can put pressure on your health, relationships and all other areas of your life, and this can mean that the pressure translates into an urgency to get the issue resolved and the IVA done as quickly as you possibly can.'

'It is crucial that you fully understand your income and expenditure, and only agree to payments that you realistically can afford. If you have even the slightest doubt about the IVA's affordability, make sure that you take a step back and consider your income and expenditure once again until you are absolutely sure that your IVA will be sustainable, even with the little glitches that life sometimes throws your way. An ill conceived IVA is extremely likely to fail some time over the period of the agreement, and this may give you even more trouble than you had in the first place.'

Steve Rees

Steve Rees is MD of Debt Management Plan firm Vincent Bond. He has been working as a debt consultant for over seven years.

'In my experience, Insolvency Practitioners can be very practical and not necessarily very friendly because they are dealing with the situation from a professional point of view. However, it is very important that the client should understand the Insolvency Practitioner is working for them, and with them, and disclose *everything*. As a debt advisor I often get calls from people who are already in IVAs and I always direct them to their Insolvency Practitioner. Don't be put off if you find the Insolvency Practitioner to be a little abrupt; put your position forward clearly and comprehensively, and carefully consider the Insolvency Practitioner's advice. This will ensure that you start off on the right foot.'

Essential advice

- Disclose every detail of your financial and personal affairs honestly and openly. The Insolvency Practitioner is there to help and advise you, not to judge you.
- Be realistic in your budgeting. Make sure you account for every cost, and that your budget for food and household expenditure is sensible and affordable.
- Take some time out to think about whether you wish to proceed; don't just sign on the dotted line immediately. Consult with family members, and get an outside opinion from someone you trust.
- Be sure that you understand and discuss overtime, windfalls and equity release in detail with your IP if they are likely to affect you.
- Don't view the five year IVA as being your only option. Bankruptcy can be perfectly viable if your disposable income isn't high enough and you aren't in a job that will be affected by it (company owner, police officer, member of the armed forces and so on).

The creditors meeting

One of the misconceptions about creditors' meetings is that it actually occurs in a physical sense. These days it is usually done by letter, email or phone; there is no actual meeting which the creditors, Insolvency Practitioner and debtor attend. Many debtors imagine that they will have to stand in front of the creditors and argue their case, but, since it is a paper meeting, the only problem that a debtor usually encounters when the creditors' meeting approaches is a sense of anxiety surrounding the outcome.

Often the result of the creditors' meeting will be modifications, which means that the creditors will agree to accept the IVA but only subject to certain conditions. If you are in a state of anxiety at the time, you will be inclined to accept them without giving them due consideration, just to ensure that the IVA is agreed. This is something that is really to be avoided – some modifications are minor, but others can be crucial changes to your proposal.

My Story

I will never forget the day of the creditors' meeting. It was cold and grey, and the rain was lashing against the windows. I had taken a day off work so that I could be perfectly prepared for what was going to happen. I spent most of the day sitting on the sofa with my wife, huddled in a duvet and drinking cups of chamomile tea and watching daytime television. We just wanted something to take our minds off the significance of the day.

Until just a few days before the meeting, I thought I would need to attend. I fully expected to be required to pull out my suit and tie once again and head down to London. But it was not to be. I just had to be near a phone. I had the phone right by my ear all day, lying on the cushion by my head. Every hour or so I would check the ringer to make sure that the volume was turned up, and occasionally I would ring the house phone from my mobile to check that it was working. But then Bev reminded me that I was engaging the line by doing that, so I stopped. Lunch-time came and went. Suddenly the phone rang.

"Hello?" I said.
"Hi Andy, Dan here." It was my brother. "Just ringing to see if you have heard about the IVA yet?"
"Not yet, Dan," I replied, trying to remain polite. "I will let you know as soon as I hear. And please don't call in the meantime, I am worried that the Insolvency Practitioner won't be able to get through."

The day wore on, and still the phone didn't ring. We had the heating off to save money, and so I got another duvet from upstairs to snuggle up for comfort. Bev and I finished the box of chamomile tea and moved on to rosehip. As we approached three o'clock, I decided to call the Insolvency Practitioner myself to see if there was any news. Just as I was about to pick up the receiver, the phone rang. I looked at Beverly and she looked at me. Then I picked it up.

"Hello?" I said.
"Hello, Andy, it's me," came my father-in-law's voice. "I was just ringing to see if there has been any news?"

"I'm afraid not, mate," I replied. "And I don't want to be rude, but we're trying to keep the line free for the Insolvency Practitioner."

"Yes, yes, of course, I do apologize. Just let me know as soon as there are any developments."

"I will, I will, thanks," I said, and put down the phone. I began to dial the Insolvency Practitioner's number.

"Hang on, love," said Beverly. "What if she's trying to get through just as we're calling her?" I paused mid-dial.

"You're right," I said, having given the matter some thought. "I'll sit down again."

Later in the afternoon I got up from the sofa and began pacing around the room. Bev shook her head and gathered the duvet around her. As I completed circuit after circuit of the sitting-room. I knew the kids would be back from school soon. The Insolvency Practitioner *had* to call soon, surely. Then, suddenly, I'd had enough.

"I'm ringing them," I said, decisively. "I'm putting my foot down."

"Are you sure that's a good idea?" she asked.

"Look, I'm doing it now and that's the end of it," I said, and dialled the number. It rang about five or six times before somebody picked up. I demanded to be transferred to the Insolvency Practitioner.

"Oh," said the voice on the other end, "you are lucky. She was just about to walk out the door and go home. Let me see if I can catch her."

"Please do," I replied. There was a scuffling noise and the Insolvency Practitioner finally came on the line. I looked at Bev, and she looked at me.

"Ah, Mr. Davie," began the Insolvency Practitioner, "I'm glad it was you. I've been trying to get hold of you all day but the phone has been engaged."

"How about the IVA? Do we know yet?"

"Yes, we do. We got the answer through a few hours ago. It's been accepted. No modifications. Straight acceptance. Well done."

I dropped the phone on the carpet, ran over to the sofa and dived onto the sofa next to Beverly, laughing like a maniac. The sofa tipped over backwards and we tumbled to the floor, all legs, arms and duvet. Both of us were laughing now. Eventually I got to my feet, untangled myself from the duvet and ran around the room cheering my head off, only stopping to drop to one knee and pump my fist back and forth. Then I put my t-shirt up over my head and did a few more laps before I tripped over Beverly and was upended onto the duvet again.

The next day, I got all the details from my Insolvency Practitioner. Apparently only American Express didn't accept the IVA, which was pretty common in those days. But that didn't matter because we only owed American Express 10% of the total, so that meant we had a 90% acceptance from the creditors. Looking back, my Insolvency Practitioner had been confident all along that the IVA would be successful, especially now that there was no house or assets involved and the case had become fairly simple. For a long time some of that confidence rubbed off on me. But I was still extremely nervous about it, so when the IVA was finally accepted straight out, with no modifications or creditor demands, I was over the moon.

IVA.co.uk Forum Members' Stories

Sarah Smith, Gloucestershire

'I was incredibly worried and anxious about what the outcome of the creditors' meeting would be. I got up and went to work in the morning as usual, trying to keep a brave face and continue with some sense of reality. Then the phone rang. It was my debt management agency saying they had incorrect information about one of my debts. My heart fell. I discussed the situation with them and soon found out it was a minor typing error...a minor typing error that added a two to the front of one of my debts. This was quickly resolved and all of the creditors agreed. I'd never felt so relieved in my life.'

IVA.co.uk Forum Experts' Advice

Mark Allen

Mark Allen is a partner in the Accountancy firm Grant Thornton, and is responsible for the National IVA Service Line. He is a chartered accountant, licensed Insolvency Practitioner and a regular panel member on the televised IVA.co.uk Debates.

'In the past, when the legislation was first put together 19 years ago, there would actually be a physical creditors' meeting. I remember it well; the creditors would sit at a table looking at the client, and I, as the Insolvency Practitioner, would sit there reading out the proposal. Nowadays, however, we don't go to the inconvenience of calling a physical creditors' meeting — only the name remains. Large creditors instruct Grant Thornton or someone else to vote on their behalf, as it were by proxy. In our representative capacity, we take instructions from creditors to vote in a particular way, according to a particular set of guidelines.'

'As soon as the meeting happens, one of my team or staff monitors the proxies as they come in, and as soon as we have enough creditors who have accepted the IVA to make it a success, we contact the client and tell them the good news.'

Melanie Giles

Melanie Giles is an independent Insolvency Practitioner and has been working in the debt solutions industry for over twenty years.

'At the creditor's meeting, the client should expect an honest appreciation of his or her proposal by creditors, and also potentially to be faced with creditor modifications. These days, with the market being as it is, there may very well be a potential increase in payments demanded by the creditors, and it is good to expect this so that you are not shocked if and when it occurs. The majority of proceedings now are done by post or fax. Debtors should take comfort in the knowledge most IVA proposals are accepted.'

'If you are unlucky enough to have your IVA proposal rejected, the first thing to do is to consider if an improved offer of settlement can be made. Carefully consider the alternatives and listen to your Insolvency Practitioner's advice. Try to talk to the creditors directly to see if there is a specific reason why the IVA was rejected.'

'Always keep in communication with your Insolvency Practitioner – you have appointed them to act for you and for that short window of your creditors meeting you should be their number one priority. If there is ever an issue with one of our IVAs, and this is very rare, I always tell my clients that we can talk about it. In larger, more process based firms the Insolvency Practitioner has very little hands-on contact with their case-load due to logistics, so it is very different in a smaller firm to a larger firm.'

Essential advice

- Be confident in your proposal. If you have worked honestly and realistically with your Insolvency Practitioner, you will be putting forward your very best offer to repay your creditors. The vast majority of IVA proposals are accepted.
- Have a pen and paper to hand so that you can note down anything important. This will help you to remember later, as you may be emotional at the time.
- Make sure that you ask your creditors to consider the outcome before accepting it. Take all the time available to you to make the decision, and think about it again in detail.
- Try to maintain a sense of perspective. The IVA can be proposed again, and there are always other options, so it is not an 'all or nothing' scenario.

Modifications to the proposal

It is very common for creditors to propose modifications at the meeting, and it is also very common for the debtor to accept these modifications without considering them carefully. Typically, these modifications will be for increased payments, but they can also concern other aspects of the IVA, such as equity release from a property.

Many people, having carefully put together a realistic proposal, lose their heads and blindly agree when they are faced with modifications. It is vital that you avoid doing this, or you are in danger of signing up to a proposal that may have been dramatically altered since you first drafted it. Most IVA budgets are drafted so tightly, even a small monthly increase in payments could be critical. You must be fully aware of the implications of any modifications before you agree to proceed.

My story

I would recommend mentally preparing yourself for receiving modifications. I've seen many people go through this process on the IVA.co.uk forums. I often hear that people get a call from their Insolvency Practitioner saying, "The IVA has been accepted, but there is just a small modification in which you need to release equity in the fourth year." Now often people are so worked up by that time – as you can tell I was – that they just accept the modification unquestioningly through pure relief. Looking back, I'm sure I would have done the same if the Insolvency Practitioner had told me that I had modifications. However, it is vitally important that you don't just accept the modifications right away, without giving them a good lot of thought. You are allowed fourteen days after the creditors' meeting to think about it and consider the modifications in your own good time. Don't worry; the creditors are not going to withdraw their offer over that period.

I strongly suggest that you use that time to think about it carefully again and again, discuss it with your partner, friends and family, and make sure you fully understand what you are agreeing to before you go ahead. For example, the equity release can be a hell of a clause. It amounts to a blank cheque to withdraw almost all the equity from your property, and you really don't know how much the equity will be in five years time.

When it comes to increased payments, you must be prepared to stick to your guns. If you've worked out your budget and how much you can realistically afford, if your creditors ask for £50 more each month, don't agree straight away just to get it through. Stop. Take your fourteen days. £50 across all your creditors may be increased revenue of only 1p in the pound or something similar for them. £50 makes a big difference to someone in an IVA – it could be the difference between make or break. It could be your petrol or clothes for the month. Negotiating over modifications is something of a grey area – sometimes you can meet a creditor half way if they ask for a payment increase. Sometimes the creditor will not budge. Talk to your Insolvency Practitioner and see if you can make a realistic counter offer.

IVA.co.uk Forum Members' Stories

Jonathan Tinsley, South Yorkshire

'When I finally got the phone call to tell me the result of the creditors' meeting, I was surprised to hear that modifications had been proposed. Although the Insolvency Practitioner had indeed mentioned it to me, there was so much new information to take on board that I don't think I really understood what it meant. Now I found out that the creditors wanted me to pay an additional £25 per month. Fortunately, I was able to prove that I couldn't afford to pay any more than was agreed on the proposal, and my IVA went ahead without the modifications.'

IVA.co.uk Forum Experts' Advice

Mark Allen
Mark Allen is a partner in the accountancy firm Grant Thornton, and is responsible for the National IVA Service Line. He is a chartered accountant, licensed Insolvency Practitioner and a regular panel member on the televised IVA.co.uk Debates.

'In many cases there are modifications made at the creditors' meeting. What that means is that the creditors might want amendments to the proposal. If this occurs, the client should expect the modifications to be explained to them by the Insolvency Practitioner in layman's language, and to be allowed sufficient time to think if he or she can live with the modified proposal or not. I have sat on a few Government 'Working Groups' to look at improvements that can be made to this area of the process, because there have been instances of misplaced expectations from the creditors, and from debtors as well. In average cases you have ten creditors, which means ten different viewpoints being brought to bear upon your proposal.'

'Part of what I have been trying to achieve recently has been the introduction of universal standards and criteria to the industry, through the British Banking Association and the Insolvency Service. You will never get all forty UK creditors to agree on everything, that would be unreasonable, but my aim is at least to get them to agree on key issues such as dealing with equity issues, income issues and so on. But even with this drive towards universality, you can still get up to ten modifications for each case, be they minor or major, so an important part of the Insolvency Practitioner's role is to explain the consequences of these clearly to the client.'

'It is becoming better than it was. If clients are not happy with the modifications, ultimately they must bear in mind that they are relying on 75% of creditors to accept the arrangement or else it will be rejected. At the end of the day, the creditors are being offered less than the original contractual sum in return, so finally it is up to them, it is their choice.'

'But there is always room for negotiation. Let's say, for example, the creditors are putting forward a modification in which they are asking for £30 per month more, because they are of the opinion that the debtor is spending too much money on food. If the client feels this is unfair, he or she can go back to the creditors via the Insolvency Practitioner, who will explain any extenuating circumstances and negotiate with the creditors. The Insolvency Practitioner will explain that the client is not happy, and then the aim will be to make every effort to reach a compromise and move forward. If no compromise is forthcoming from the side of the creditors, however, then the IVA will end up being rejected. In such a scenario the debtor is not financially worse off, but there has been a monumental waste of time, and the debtor is back to square one.'

Steve Rees

Steve Rees is MD of Debt Management Plan firm Vincent Bond. He has been working as a debt consultant for over seven years.

'What you want to hear is that your IVA is accepted; you don't want to be faced with modifications or a rejection. However, in reality this is not necessarily the end of the world. Even if your IVA is rejected you can propose it again if you make a material change to your proposal. Other options are Bankruptcy or a Debt Management Plan, which doesn't resolve the situation permanently but can be a useful stop-gap. I have seen Debt Management Plans that are supposed to last 25 or 30 years. How can that possibly be realistic, both for the debtor and the creditors? But a DMP can give you some breathing space. Before long you may find that your circumstances have changed and you can either pay the debt back in full or propose an IVA again.

'The key thing to remember here is that you are essentially on the back foot; you are asking your creditors to agree to accept less than you have contractually agreed, because of A, B or C reason. But even though the banks have a duty of care to the client and an obligation to be reasonable, ultimately it is down to their discretion as to whether or not they will accept your proposal. One current issue that is being hotly debated is whether or not the banks are being fair in the way they operate. There are some banks who only accept a minimum dividend of 40p in the pound. If that's the case and the debtor is willing to sell his or her home and make other serious sacrifices, and still only getting to 35p, and the creditor says no because of the hurdle rate of 40p, there are many who would view this as unfair and unreasonable. I don't think the issue will go away, any time soon.'

Essential advice

- Use the entirety of the time available to consider your position before you accept any modifications.
- If your Insolvency Practitioner hasn't explained the implications of the modifications with sufficient clarity, don't be afraid to ask for more information.
- If for any reason you are not happy with the modifications, communicate this to your Insolvency Practitioner and stick to your guns. There is often a compromise that can be reached.
- It is better to have a realistic IVA proposal rejected than it is to have an impossible one accepted. There will always be other options to consider.

Remortgaging and equity release

If you are a homeowner, it is very important to be fully informed of the demands that an IVA makes on your property. Although unlike Bankruptcy the IVA allows you to remain in control of your property, it usually requires you to release all the available equity in the form of a remortgage, and offer the lump sum to the creditors. Thus you must resign yourself to the fact that you will inevitably leave the IVA without any unsecured debt, but without significant equity in your property either. There are advantages to this, chief of which is that equity release often enables you to settle your IVA early. However, if you are not fully aware of the rules, the equity release can come as a nasty shock.

My story

Luckily, after three years I was able to settle my IVA early. During my IVA, we actually managed to buy a house with money that my mother gave us as a deposit. Our mortgage repayments were the same as our previous rent, so it didn't affect our IVA from that point of view. We bought it six or seven months into the IVA, and within two years the property prices in the area had shot up and the equity had become pretty substantial due to this increase. I asked questions on forums, trying to get advice from people regarding the best course of action. By that time I had started to rely more on the IVA.co.uk community forum for information than the Insolvency Practitioner! I was concerned because the last thing I wanted was for the Insolvency Practitioner to demand all the equity on behalf of the creditors and still have to make monthly payments for the full five years. So before speaking to the Insolvency Practitioner, I was very cunning. I did a lot of on IVA.co.uk, and looking online, and scouring my original documents for information.

Eventually I was 95% sure that the equity could be used as an early settlement offer. I wrote to my Insolvency Practitioner and asked how much the minimum settlement offer would be. I knew that if I went the full course of monthly payments I would end up paying back twenty thousand pounds, so I expected the early settlement to be a little lower than that. But when it finally came through, it was twenty three thousand. By that time, however, I was so desperate to have the thing over and done with that I went right ahead.

I found a company on the Internet that was able to offer me a mortgage and release the required equity; to settle the IVA early. I got myself a mortgage offer and went back to the Insolvency Practitioner. She convened a creditors' meeting, and instantly my offer was accepted by all the creditors, every single one. I can still remember I had lots of congratulations posted on the forum. I was getting paid a few days after the IVA concluded, and as I didn't need to make any more payments I could keep all the money I had earned – every single penny.

An IVA is a serious five-year agreement, which affects your whole life. This is especially the case when there are houses involved – you might be agreeing to forsake all the equity that may grow in your property over a five-year period, which may end up being fairly substantial. So it is vital that you fully understand the implications of what you are getting into, and for this reason it is very important that you have an Insolvency Practitioner behind you who you know you can fully rely on to be easily accessible, supportive and knowledgeable. If you use it carefully, equity in a property can be a valuable asset for someone in an IVA, particularly if you can use it to offer a Full and Final settlement.

IVA.co.uk Forum Members' Stories

Angela Pole, Leicester

'My equity proved to be a great advantage when it came to proposing an IVA. My Insolvency Practitioner advised me that equity release would be central to my proposal right from the beginning when we first had a face-to-face meeting. The Insolvency Practitioner was excellent – very professional yet friendly at the same time – and said that as I had equity to the value of more than 25% of my total unsecured debt, I could offer a 'full-and-final settlement' to my creditors by way of a remortgage. This meant that all I had to do was release a lump sum from my house and the remaining unsecured debt would be written off, without the need for monthly payments! I was overjoyed at the prospect of having all my debts sorted out in one fell swoop, and we made the proposal.'

'It took weeks to arrange, searching around through mortgage brokers to find someone who could offer us a bigger mortgage to raise the equity. This meant, of course that we went onto a higher interest rate on our mortgage, and we'll have to remain on it for some years to come. It hasn't been easy, but it was the best thing that we could have done.'

IVA.co.uk Forum Experts' Advice

Melanie Giles

Melanie Giles is an independent Insolvency Practitioner and has been working in the debt solutions industry for over twenty years.

'Remortgaging is the most important thing you are going to be asked to do in an IVA, and the implications of getting this wrong, or not understanding what you are required to do, could well affect your home.'

'You will be required to explore the possibility of releasing equity during the final year of your IVA, not knowing how the house prices will rise and what mortgages will be available. This can equate to a black cloud hanging over the debtor, but in today's current economic climate, post "credit-crunch" the lack of funding available to persons with an impaired credit rating could work in your favour. And in any case further lending is limited to a maximum of 85% loan to value with affordability of the new mortgage payments to be limited to 50% of the current IVA monthly payments.'

Steve Rees

Steve Rees is MD of Debt Management Plan firm Vincent Bond. He has been working as a debt consultant for over seven years.

'In my opinion, equity release is always going to be worth it. Of course, if you have enough equity to negotiate a full and final settlement, that is the best solution as you don't have to go through years of budgeting restrictions. However, even if your equity release occurs some time into the IVA, it can allow the IVA to conclude early.'

'It is important to maintain your sense of perspective; although you will be giving up your equity, overall you are far better off because the creditors are writing a lot of money off in return. If you were to go bankrupt you would lose the property anyway, so the IVA usually presents a good deal.'

Essential advice

- If you are a homeowner, discuss the issue of your equity exhaustively with your Insolvency Practitioner as early as possible.
- Always keep the bigger picture in mind, which is that in the long run you will have debt written off and be free from the burden of monthly payments.
- Keep track of the equity in your property, including changes in local house prices.
- Ask your IP about the option of a full and final settlement – it may be that you can afford it by supplementing your income with money from family or friends.

Chapter Four:

Making your IVA a success

If you are seriously thinking about entering an IVA, you must consider what measures you will take to ensure its success. Five years is a long time, and once you have signed up for the IVA you can't simply back out. Before taking the plunge and submitting an IVA proposal, do your research, review the material in this chapter, and create a personal strategy for IVA success.

Life in an IVA

Most people have got used to the fact that they have a credit card in their back pocket, just in case they need a bit of extra cash. When you're in an IVA, this is not possible. Although there are checks and balances in place to allow for the unexpected, in an IVA you have committed to paying a set amount every month. This has to become a priority, which means that far more attention has to be paid to budgeting. You need to be able to plan well in advance for yearly expenses such as Christmas and car servicing, as well as building an emergency fund to take care of unexpected expense. This is something that most people, especially those in serious debt, are not familiar with – it means putting a little money aside over several months or a year in order to provide for those one-off events, and this takes a large degree of organisation, discipline and self-restraint.

The budget that you will be living on will be tight. The creditors need to feel assured that you genuinely are making every reasonable effort to pay them back, and this means not spending money on luxuries. Many people in IVAs have to rely on family help for things like holidays or go without as there is no allowance in the IVA budget for these. The effect that this budgeting has on you will depend to a great extent on your circumstances; some people in serious debt have become accustomed to pinching the pennies whereas others have been living the high life to the end. In my experience, almost everyone will find the IVA budget a bit of a squeeze.

As I found out to my cost, it is common for companies and Insolvency Practitioners to change their behavior once the IVA has been accepted. Once the IVA has been accepted, many companies make you to deal with a case manager from then on, rather than the Insolvency Practitioner him or herself. In fact, during the course of my IVA I had two or three different case managers. They are often not particularly highly trained – at one point, through my knowledge on the IVA.co.uk forum I felt I knew more than the person dealing with the case! I found that once my IVA was accepted, trying to get an answer or contact from my Insolvency Practitioner was very hard, and I often felt completely helpless.

Once the IVA has been set up you can't back out without serious consequences. The Insolvency Practitioner will have been paid relatively soon after the IVA has begun, so they have little incentive to give you their time. It is more financially viable for them to direct their efforts at securing new business, since the old business can't go away for fear of Bankruptcy. I have come across this on the IVA.co.uk community forum, particularly with larger companies. If you ask a question of them that you really want answering, you end may have to chase and this can be incredibly frustrating and time consuming. All of this points to the advantages of using a smaller company who may be better placed to offer you the kind of care you will need.

If at all possible, get a direct line for your Insolvency Practitioner – not to answer every single question of course, but for the major things such as ascertaining a reasonable settlement figure or a critical change in circumstance. For those kinds of make-or-break issues you really want to speak to the Insolvency Practitioner directly. So long as you make sure they understand that you are not going to trouble them regarding minor issues, there should be no reason why they would not give you a number for their direct line. I have heard of people waiting up to two or three weeks for the Insolvency Practitioner to get back to them, which is absolutely shocking considering the importance of the issues at stake. If the Insolvency Practitioner is unhelpful, difficult to get hold of, or unprofessional, this will have a profound effect on your life. You run the risk of having calls unanswered, your concerns not properly addressed, and your IVA poorly managed. That's why finding a good IP is vital.

My story

In my case, the ecstasy of having no more hassle from creditors and a light at the end of the tunnel was short-lived. At first, I felt totally overjoyed – I was constantly grinning, and everyone kept asking me why I was so happy. I can only compare it to the experience of having a new baby; you are in a state of bliss, and nobody can quite work out the reason why.

But then the time came around when I had to write out the first IVA cheque, for £450. As I was writing it I felt split down the middle. On the one hand the figure that I was writing on the cheque was less than half of the amount that I had been shelling out to all my different creditors until then. It was great knowing that I only had to make one payment, and that the creditors would not be able to contact me ever again. I had this feeling that there was an endgame – every payment I made was a step towards debt freedom, and there were only sixty steps – it didn't seem too bad at all. But then, on the other hand, I was also rather apprehensive. The problem was, in my bank I only had £500 left. So that meant that for the remaining two weeks of the month all I had to live on, for myself and the family, was what we had in our pockets – which amounted to £50 – and the £50 left in the bank. That was a grand total of one hundred pounds; a hundred quid for a family of six to live off for two weeks? The notion filled me with dread, and rightly so.

I mentioned it to Beverly immediately. This in itself was an improvement, since before the IVA I was in the habit of keeping financial worries to myself and not sharing anything with her. I was expecting her to panic, to flip out. But she didn't, she was very calm and collected.

"Oh dear," she said, "we must have gone overboard with our spending somewhere along the line. I think we should have been a bit more careful to monitor our budget as we went, don't you?"

"I suppose you're right," I admitted, "but what can we do now? That's the question. We can't live on a hundred quid for the rest of the month."

In the end we made a humiliating phone call to my father-in-law, who agreed to lend us some money. He paid £200 directly into my account that very day, and we were back on track – or so we thought. I remember as I withdrew the money I still felt torn in two. I was happy that we hadn't come a cropper in the very first month of the IVA. On the other hand, I felt downcast and extremely disappointed in myself. This was meant to be a new start for all of us – we were supposed to have drawn a line in the sand and left the days of debt behind us. What on earth were we doing borrowing money from my father-in-law right after making our first ever IVA payment? I decided that I would make a stronger effort next month to budget properly, and make sure that we were living within our means.

But that was only the beginning. At the start of the next month, as soon as I got paid I made sure that I paid back my father-in-law in full. The problem was, that then caused a knock-on effect and I ended up having to borrow from him yet again at the end of the following month. So the spiral began – always having to turn to friends or family members for acts of charity just to get by. I think it was several months before it finally dawned on me what had happened. If it wasn't for making those over-ambitious cutbacks of £200 in my expenses in the first place, we would have been able to manage fine. But there was nothing for it. We had committed ourselves to the IVA, and we had to see it out for the duration. There was nothing to be done apart from to get our heads down and struggle on.

It was no walk in the park. Looking back with the benefit of hindsight, there is always something that crops up somewhere along the line that you haven't accounted for in your expenses, be it an unexpected school trip or replacing the washing machine. Most IVAs can absorb such small glitches by temporarily cutting back other expenses, or using money that has been put aside for a rainy day. However, in my case those kinds of small problems made all the difference; it was exceptionally hard because of the incorrect income and expenditure that we had agreed in the beginning.

The first few months were the hardest, I think, because we all had to adjust to a whole different way of life. For a heavy credit card user like myself, the idea that I could not use another credit card to fill the odd gap here and there for an entire five years was an absolute shock to the system. When we went shopping at the supermarket –

using the supermarket where I now worked meant that we had a bit of a staff discount – we could no longer just get what we used to get. We had to get the basic, budget version of everything and go without all luxuries, even the smallest treat. As soon as the IVA started, when I went shopping I would typically do so with my last £100 we had.

There were times when I had to put things back at the check-out because my money would not stretch enough to cover everything I had chosen. That was extremely embarrassing, especially as the staff all knew me at the supermarket. The funny thing was that all the staff thought I was a real scrooge because they thought I was making a lot of money. Of course, they didn't know anything about the IVA, or the fact that I was trying to pay all my bills, feed and clothe four kids, and also spare £450 per month for the IVA. I also seemed richer because I had the use of a nice company car, which meant that the staff at the supermarket saw me driving around in this flashy car, and then buying all the economy food at the supermarket on a tight budget. It was humiliating at first. Later on, of course, I got used to it. I simply asked the check-out operator to budget my shopping as I went, and I would leave things at the checkout if need be.

As time went on things went from bad to worse. There were days on which I couldn't even afford lunch, and I had to go hungry, pretending that I was working too hard to take a lunch break. If I had to attend a meeting at a different store or offices, I had to worry whether or not there was enough diesel in car. Although the car was provided by the company, I had to buy my own diesel. As a result I used to run the car on the orange light a lot. I knew within one or two miles how much I could get out of the dribble of fuel that remained. Often I ended up running it all the way to empty – and beyond.

Luckily the kids adjusted quickly. We had downsized from a big house to a small rented place, and initially I thought that this might be a challenge for the children. They used to have their own rooms when we were in our old place, but when we moved they had to go back to sleeping in bunk beds. I have to hand it to them, they just accepted it without any problems at all. My son used to work alongside me on a Saturday in the store, and I remember that we used to laugh about the fact that he had more money than me – and he was only 16!

Our social lives were affected too. When I got home in the evening, I had nothing to do apart from watch the TV, as going out cost too much money. And the same applied when I was lucky enough to get a few days off. With no money there was almost no point in having time off in the first place. There was nothing do apart from sit about at home. So I thought that I might as well fill the time with work. In a way, I was trying to deal with the situation by burying myself in my job. I managed to get a promotion and a small pay rise, which eased things somewhat; my IVA contributions became a little more manageable.

At first, not going on holiday was tough – we just couldn't afford it. It made me feel really depressed not to have something to look forward to, and not to have anything exciting to share with the children. Luckily, my workaholic habits won me some holiday vouchers in the first year of the IVA. For two weeks we had a lovely time in Florida, and I felt a whole lot better when I returned.

After this, every now and again my father-in-law and my mum would club together and pay for us to go on holiday. They would both come along with us, and that was really something to go for in the future, like a milestone that we would try and aim for.

Bev was very, very good during that period. If your partner is not on board, I reckon you're never going to make it. She stuck by me all the way. Her time at home was quite long and tedious because she didn't work at the time, she was just looking after the kids, so that meant that there was a lot of time to chew things over, and a lot she could potentially have complained about. But she was supportive all the way through, she was brilliant. The fact that we could see the end of the tunnel kept us going.

It's not wise to see the IVA as a quick fix. It is true that you will have a considerable portion of your debt written off, but this is not the whole story. The IVA is only good for people who genuinely are stuck down a hole, are willing to make every conceivable effort to put things right and are happy to make sacrifices in the process, and as my experience shows, it is crucial to get your budget right from the very beginning.

IVA.co.uk Forum Members' Stories

Stephen Parry, Wales

'During my time in the IVA I found the budgeting side of things quite hard. We had never lived a flamboyant lifestyle but we were comfortable. Once we were in the IVA we had to budget very carefully to make sure we didn't overspend, and if we felt like an evening out we knew we could only spend a certain amount, anything else would have its consequences.'

Dominic Corby, London

'To be honest, I found budgeting very easy – it was the least of my worries! One reason for this was that just before the creditors' meeting I happened to have a pay-rise, and I had to wait until my annual review to reassess my expenditure. This meant that I had a bit more cash every month, and I didn't experience much financial hardship. Regardless of what payments you agree in the initial IVA proposal, poor budgeting can make any IVA unmanageable. It is essential to learn how to manage your money.'

IVA.co.uk Forum Experts' Advice

James Falla

James Falla is the Director of the debt help company Thomas Charles, and has advised people who have personal debt problems since 1997.

'You should not expect your IVA to be easy – the way to make sure you get through it is to keep your head down and focus on the goal at the end. Always think to yourself, "This is not going to last forever." Insolvency is not a small problem, and it will not go away overnight; it requires a comprehensive solution, which will take a years to take full effect.

'If you're in an IVA, you must be in complete control of your monthly budget. It does surprise me when people in an IVA can't lay a hand on their Income and Expenditure budget quickly. Your IVA proposal will show the expenses and income you signed up to, and this should be clear to you at all times so that you can structure your spending accordingly. You must have a clear view in your mind of what your budget is from day one. After a while it will become habit, and eventually it will be second nature. By the time the IVA ends you will probably have become a saver!'

'There are no specific budgeting tips for those who are in IVAs. Just budget. The best way to get through the IVA process is to keep a money diary. You should write exactly how much you have coming in, the direct debits you will have to pay, and how much money you will have available to spend each week.

'You should never find yourself in a situation where you find yourself with an IVA you can't pay – Andy Davie's experience is sobering. Don't enter into the IVA if you won't be able to maintain the payments. It is becoming increasingly difficult to change the IVA once you're in it. These days, some creditors say that you can't change the IVA proposal for 24 months. If you do encounter unexpected changes in your circumstances, speak to the Insolvency Practitioner about it. If it is genuinely beyond your control, they can request a variation from the creditors. Getting the variation accepted depends entirely on whether or not the creditors are in agreement. Some tend to be reluctant to agree in the early years.'

Melanie Giles

Melanie Giles is an independent Insolvency Practitioner and has been working in the debt solutions industry for over twenty years.

'The most important advice for those going into an IVA is to keep the Supervisor fully up-to-date and advised of all changes in circumstances. You should really try to maintain regular payments without missing any, and advise the Supervisor as soon as you feel unable to make the payments, giving a clear reason why. Make sure that you respond to all requests for further information promptly.'

'Most importantly of all, don't take out more credit without the supervisor's permission. I once had a client who bought a car without my permission because he had a pay-rise and felt that he deserved a treat. The problem was that he purchased the car on hire purchase.

When we had the annual review the hire purchase repayment was declared, of which I had known nothing about. That meant that he was in default of his agreement, and I had to rapidly draw this to creditors attention and seek their agreement to the borrowings on a retrospective basis.'

'You do get the occasional repeat offender. I had a call some time ago from clients who had completed a full and final IVA with me four years ago. They had got in trouble again and wanted to do the same thing. But this is fairly unusual. Most people get used to the lifestyle by the time the five years are up, get clever at budgeting and choose to save the extra money that previously was being contributed to the IVA to fund things like holidays and home improvements.'

'If you are finding your IVA payments difficult, work out a revised budget to identify where you are overspending, discuss your problems with your Supervisor and consider if Bankruptcy is a more viable solution. I have had a few clients over the years who have thrown in the towel because they were not able to accept the level of scrutiny in an IVA. Importantly, if something goes wrong in the IVA and you feel unhappy, inform the Supervisor or seek independent financial advice. Don't ignore the issue; it will not go away.'

'In general, the best tips for budgeting couldn't be simpler. Set a monthly budget and stick to it. Pay as many bills monthly as possible instead of quarterly so you know where you are month to month. Open a savings account and place all contingency money in there for emergencies. Don't impulse buy. You should consider bulk buying and Internet shopping, which can produce significant savings.'

'Other tips that can help you budget effectively are to ensure that contingency money is set aside in a separate account, such as for car and home maintenance. Put aside your 50% of overtime into a separate account as well, to cover holidays, Christmas spending or birthdays. If you smoke, use the opportunity to cut down or quit altogether. When I told one particular client how much she was spending on cigarettes she was flabbergasted. It was one of her biggest household expenditures. She hadn't multiplied it for the month, so didn't really understand just how much smoking was costing her. The clearer you are in your own head with regard to your budgeting, the more successful your IVA will inevitably be.'

Essential advice

- Keep your IVA proposal close to hand, and use this as the basis for your monthly budget.
- Include a savings amount in this budget so that you have something to turn to for unforeseen expenses, and plan well in advance for big yearly expenses like Christmas or family birthdays.
- Buy a money diary to keep track of how much money you have left each month.
- Arrange to pay bills monthly rather than quarterly. Set up your direct debits so that you pay your IVA payment and your bills as soon as your wages come in each month.
- Research money management schemes like Thinkbanking which will allow you to tightly monitor and control your cash flow.
- Ensure that you have your Insolvency Practitioner's direct line for emergencies.
- Keep focused on the finishing line – look on each payment you make as a step towards a debt free life.

Running into trouble

There are many ways in which your IVA may run into trouble. Considering the fact that the IVA asks you to live on a tight budget with no credit for five years, it is only to be expected that there will be one or two glitches along the way. The most common problems are an unexpected expense or a sudden loss of income. Either of these can force you to miss an IVA payment, and it is vital to have advance knowledge of what can be done in this situation. Building up savings through careful budgeting can help with many problems, but sometimes the expense will be too much. The key to resolving these issues is, as you might expect, to be fully aware of the IVA protocol and to keep your Insolvency Practitioner informed. If a payment is missed, it may be possible to take a payment holiday and add it on to the end of the IVA. If there is a change in circumstances, such as reduced wages or an increase in rent, the IP can arrange a variation meeting and try to reduce the IVA payments.

My story

Things didn't go all that smoothly throughout my IVA period; quite a few things went wrong. At the start of the IVA we were on tax credits, and the tax credit people mistakenly paid it into a Lloyds TSB account that was being closed down as part of the IVA. Trying to get that money back from Lloyds TSB took months and months. In the end I had to threaten a complaint to the financial Ombudsman, and that seemed to sort things out. Once Lloyds TSB received that threat, they returned my money to me quick smart! But it was a real struggle. The Insolvency Practitioner got involved but she couldn't work on the case beyond a certain point because she was charging on a Time Cost basis, so the more time she put into recovering this money, the higher her fees would go; that meant that there was a point where her fees would overshadow the amount of money recovered.

The other main problem with the IVA as I experienced it was that my Insolvency Practitioner really wasn't particularly efficient. I had absolutely no correspondence from her, no confirmation that they were receiving the cheques that I was religiously sending out month by month. Because of this lack of contact I ended up going into three months' worth of arrears over the space of a year. When money is extremely tight and you are hearing nothing from the Insolvency Practitioner, you tend to lose your discipline. You think, "If they haven't said anything after not receiving this money, I've got away with it." It's stupid, but it's just human nature.

What happened as a result was a disaster. The Insolvency Practitioner decreed that the IVA had to run for an extra eighteen months. Eighteen months! That really knocked me flat. Just imagine how I felt – I had been in the IVA for two years already, and it had been incredibly difficult because of the too-tight budget; now it was going to be extended! It was like I had just been flushing money down the toilet all that time. Luckily I managed to negotiate an early settlement. Otherwise we would never have made it, I'm sure of that.

When I looked into the reason for the extension, it emerged that in addition to the arrears, there was a complicated car loan situation – the balance had turned out to be ten thousand pounds rather than five thousand. To make matters worse, my Insolvency

Practitioner was on a fee system called Time Cost Charging, which means that the fees were not set in stone at the beginning of the IVA, but were paid according to the amount of time they spent on my case. And because of the arrears and the car loan complications, their fees had increased as well.

Fortunately, Time Cost Charging is a thing of the past. These days all Insolvency Practitioner fees are fixed for the full five years, so you don't need to worry about the uncertainty in the way that I had to. Because of the Time Cost system I ended up paying sixteen thousand pounds in fees alone over the three years. By today's standards, that is outrageous – an Insolvency Practitioner will typically charge between six and ten thousand pounds *over the entire IVA period*, which is usually five years, regardless of whether or not the case involves complications.

The IVA in general is a very good way of repaying as much as you can afford, and it gives the creditors a much better return than Bankruptcy would. But you need to avoid making the same mistakes that I did. The key thing really is that knowledge is power. I would encourage absolutely everybody who is considering the IVA as a solution to make full use of the resources available to them at IVA.co.uk. I wish that when I went through it I had had the benefit of the forum, but it wasn't around back then. Knowledge is vitally important. If you have it, you are not frightened. But if you don't know or fully understand the ins and outs, you are put in a position of total reliance on the Insolvency Practitioner and their staff, as I was.

Jonathan Tinsley, South Yorkshire

'My IVA went very well at first, but through mistakes in budgeting I found myself unable to make one of the payments. I was quite worried about this and phoned my Insolvency Practitioner straight away. They agreed with me to let that payment pass, and then add on an extra payment at the end of the arrangement, but they made it very clear that this must not happen again. It was not until I was actually in the IVA that I realized that the payments can vary due to pay rises, overtime, and other unknown factors. I wish I would have researched it more thoroughly before going ahead.'

IVA.co.uk Forum Experts' Advice

Mark Allen

Mark Allen is a partner in the accountancy firm Grant Thornton, and is responsible for the National IVA Service Line. He is a chartered accountant, licensed Insolvency Practitioner and a regular panel member on the televised IVA.co.uk Debates.

'If you find that something goes wrong during your IVA, you should speak to the Insolvency Practitioner as soon as you are able. The Insolvency Practitioner will have a team of people working with him or her, so you should always be able to contact one of them if not the Insolvency Practitioner directly. You should explain the situation as honestly and clearly as you can. Maybe there has been a permanent reduction in income, house prices have gone up, you find that you have equity you didn't have before, you feel that you want to do a quick settlement with a lump sum that a relative has suddenly left you, or whatever. The most important thing to do is to go to the Insolvency Practitioner and explain the situation. The Insolvency Practitioner may be able to do a new deal for you.'

'In a worst case scenario, for example if you have a permanent job loss right at the beginning of the IVA period, the case would probably fail. Although the rules would suggest that Bankruptcy would follow a failed IVA, over the last two or three years the fashion has moved away from this. The reason is that the creditors have begun to appreciate if they refrain from punishing the debtor through Bankruptcy proceedings, they may be able to pursue the debt further and in this way recover more of the money they are owed.'

'All too often IVAs run into trouble as a result of a souring relationship between the client and the Insolvency Practitioner. At the start of the journey the client tends to view the Insolvency Practitioner as their guardian angel. Two years later, however, the Insolvency Practitioner suddenly gets seen as the debt collector! The problem is that first the Insolvency Practitioner is helping the client, putting them into a repayment plan for five years. But then the Insolvency Practitioner is obliged to monitor the payment plan for the whole sixty months, and clients can often resent that. So it is important for the client to maintain a sense of perspective, and not to blame the Insolvency Practitioner for doing their job.'

Melanie Giles

Melanie Giles is an independent Insolvency Practitioner and has been working in the debt solutions industry for over twenty years.

'95% of the hundreds of IVAs I have supervised have clients who have managed to budget and maintain their required payments just fine. But there is, and will always be, a small minority of clients who are simply not prepared to change their lifestyles. Over one in four IVAs in the UK fail, often because people are not prepared to deal with the reality of what is required.'

'What clients often fail to realize is that under the terms of the IVA they are still under strict supervision and their lives are still under scrutiny. Once clients have forgotten all about the creditors, and the Insolvency Practitioner is saying that they are going to increase the payments, the Insolvency Practitioner turns from the white knight to the bad guy (or girl!).'

'At the same time, the problem is not always with the individual. The client can expect the right to open communication from the Insolvency Practitioner. Particularly in larger firms, you can see Insolvency Practitioners not returning calls or clients complaining about no correspondence. There is a duty of care and open communication, and you must check an Insolvency Practitioner's reputation before instructing them.'

Essential advice

- Make sure you understand the demands an IVA places on your life, and what 'safety-valves' are in place in case of an unforeseen problem.
- If you run into short term trouble, you may be able to arrange a payment holiday, whereby you can miss one or two monthly payments which be added on to the end of the IVA.
- If you experience a change in circumstance that renders your IVA unaffordable, ask your Insolvency Practitioner to arrange a variation meeting to lower your monthly payments.
- Communicate with your Insolvency Practitioner as soon as a problem starts to occur, rather than wait until it has grown out of control. If you are going to miss a payment, you must tell your Insolvency Practitioner as far in advance as possible.
- Ensure that you don't blame your Insolvency Practitioner when they monitor your case in accordance with the IVA rules; at the same time, you can expect prompt communication and professionalism from them.

Making a complaint

Unfortunately, in a small number of cases it may be appropriate to lodge a complaint about the Insolvency Practitioner's conduct. These instances are few and far between, and the vast majority of Insolvency Practitioners do a good job. However it is empowering for the client to understand that there is a procedure for complaints if appropriate, and the threat of a complaint can sometimes be effective in galvanising a slow to respond Insolvency Practitioner into replying to your queries. In reality, all Insolvency Practitioners are subject to license laws, and if their unprofessional conduct were to lead to their license being revoked, they would lose their livelihood. For this reason they will often react positively if it is clear that you are fully aware of the sort of service you have the right to expect. If you are starting to have problems with your Insolvency Practitioner, make sure you keep a record of any correspondence – by phone, post or email – that you have with them or their company.

According to the Insolvency Practitioners Association (IPA) guidelines, grounds for complaint are "negligence, misconduct or other liability in relation to an insolvency or other professional matter, any breach of any of the IPA Articles, Rules, Regulations or Guidance or any conduct or practice likely to bring discredit upon him/herself, the IPA and its membership or the insolvency profession." Of course, this is a wide-ranging definition and this is intentional, since 'negligence' and 'misconduct' can take an almost infinite variety of forms. Based on the information in this section, if you feel that your Insolvency Practitioner is acting in a manner that may be negligent or in breach of professional conduct, the best advice would be to seek advice from any of the Insolvency Practitioner regulatory bodies. These include: the Association of Chartered Certified Accountants, the Institute of Chartered Accountants in England and Wales, the International Federation of Accountants, the Insolvency Practices Council, the Insolvency Practitioners Association, or the Insolvency Service.

If a complaint is upheld, the consequences can be serious. The Insolvency Practitioner may have his or her licence revoked, in which case he or she would no longer be able to practice within the profession. In extreme cases criminal proceedings may be launched. Lesser penalties involve an official reprimand and the issuing of a fine. From the debtor's point of view, a successful complaint can entail the receipt of compensation, the re-opening and possible overturning of a decision, and a restructuring of the IVA in order to move it forward. Such arrangements will depend on the particular circumstances of the professional misconduct and the IVA.

My story

I never made a formal complaint about my Insolvency Practitioner, despite the problems I had. I simply was not aware that such a complaint could be made, and I am not usually the sort of person to make complaints. Looking back, there is one case where a complaint might have been appropriate.

Shortly after we had started the IVA, my mother offered me money to put down as a deposit for a small house. I wanted to keep my nose clean, so I made sure that I spoke to the Insolvency

Practitioner first to ask her permission, and she said it wouldn't be a problem. She gave me a reference to offer to a new mortgage company, we moved, and everything was fine. Then, three or four months later, the Insolvency Practitioner wrote to me saying that since I am a homeowner and didn't declare it at the beginning, I could go to prison for not declaring my assets! I wasn't too worried by this because I knew they'd got it wrong, but it had a horrible effect on Beverly.

I rang them up and said, "You gave me the reference for the mortgage company! How can you say that I didn't declare the asset to you?" It was OK in the end, but the whole experience was a bit of a shock, especially for Bev. Their excuse was that I had informed them of my change of address but not that I had actually gone ahead and made the purchase. Looking back, I am pretty sure they were just trying to come up with any excuse to hide the fact that they had made a silly and unprofessional mistake. Considering the distress that such negligence can cause, I think I should have lodged a complaint, at least with the Insolvency Practitioner's company, if not the regulatory body.

IVA.co.uk Forum Members' Stories

Jonathan Tinsley, South Yorkshire

'There was only one occasion on which I considered making a complaint. My Insolvency Practitioner was simply not replying to any of my emails or phone calls. In the end I think I sent twenty emails, and received not a single reply. Then I mentioned that I was thinking of making a complaint to the regulatory body, and the following day I received an email back. I think it is shocking that I had to go that far to get decent service.'

IVA.co.uk Forum Experts' Advice

Mark Allen

Mark Allen is a partner in the accountancy firm Grant Thornton, and is responsible for the National IVA Service Line. He is a chartered accountant, licensed Insolvency Practitioner and a regular panel member on the televised IVA.co.uk Debates.

'If you are not happy with your Insolvency Practitioner, first of all you should speak to them and tell them you are unhappy with the advice or service you have received. The Insolvency Practitioner will probably have a pool of people working for him or her, and if one of them is giving bad advice or not getting back to clients quick enough, the Insolvency Practitioner needs to know so that something can be done about it. Some of the best feedback I get is from clients. The chances are that you have been dealing with a member of the Insolvency Practitioner's staff rather than the Insolvency Practitioner him or herself, so if you think they are not reliable, or abrupt on the phone or whatever – tell them.'

'For serious complaints you can go to the regulatory body. We Insolvency Practitioners study and work hard to get our licenses, which means that we don't want to get them revoked. The Insolvency Practitioner is legally obliged to give you details of the relevant regulatory body, and I can tell you that they take complaints very seriously indeed.'

Steve Rees

Steve Rees is MD of Debt Management Plan firm Vincent Bond. He has been working as a debt consultant for over seven years.

'It is important for the debtor to be clear about the kind of service that can be reasonably expected from an Insolvency Practitioner. The Insolvency Practitioner is there to give advice, make clear the available options, and advise the client to pursue the IVA only if it is the most appropriate course of action. The Insolvency Practitioner should never force the client into anything.'

'In a sense the Insolvency Practitioner occupies a dual role – they respond to client in their own interest, but also to the creditors in their interest; don't forget, it is the creditors who are paying for the service at the end of the day. The fees that Insolvency Practitioners take are reducing the money the banks get, so in effect the banks are paying their salaries. As such, they have a definite duty to the creditors. If the creditors think the Insolvency Practitioner is lying to them, or the debtor is, they will reject the IVA. So they need to have faith that the Insolvency Practitioner is doing a good job.'

'It is the Insolvency Practitioner's responsibility to put together a realistic proposal to the creditors. If the debtor wants to pay less, it is the Insolvency Practitioner's duty to say to them that is not going to happen unless there is a genuine reason for it; contributions must be raised in accordance with guidelines. The reason for this is that if these guidelines are not adhered to, the IVA will be rejected. Of course, this may not be what the debtor wants to hear, but it is important to recognize that the role of the Insolvency Practitioner is such that he or she must act in the interests of both parties, and offer professional and impartial advice.'

'If you find that your Insolvency Practitioner is providing consistently poor service, or you feel you have been seriously misadvised, it might be worth considering lodging a complaint. Write to them first, allowing an appropriate length of time for response. Then arrange to meet if there's no luck. The next step is to find out if the firm has a complaints procedure. Write to the senior partner or head of operations. If the issue is still not resolved, you should then take advice from an alternative Insolvency Practitioner or insolvency experienced lawyer. As last resort, refer to the Insolvency Practitioners regulatory body.'

Essential advice

- Bring up any instances of poor professional conduct with the Insolvency Practitioner, or their staff, as soon as they occur. Keep track of all communications you have with the firm.
- Try to get a matter resolved informally before resorting to a formal complaint. Lodge your complaint with the company first – only if their response is unsatisfactory should you go to the regulatory body.
- Be aware of the role that the Insolvency Practitioner is supposed to fulfil before judging whether or not their behaviour is inappropriate.
- Be aware of the channels of complaint, and what constitutes a valid complaint.

Finishing the IVA

Once the last payment for your IVA has been made, it is the Insolvency Practitioner's job to officially conclude the arrangements and issue you with a certificate of completion. This might seem like a formality, but it is a vital part of the process and must be done quickly. The issue here is that the case does not go off the register until it is officially closed. In such a case, the real danger is that the 'windfall provision' is there for as long as the case is open. Even though the IVA may be completed, if it hasn't been closed by the Insolvency Practitioner and removed from the register, the creditors still have the right to grab any windfall that might come your way, even though they no longer have the right to demand monthly payments from the client any more. That puts you in an extremely vulnerable position, and if money were to suddenly turn up the creditors would be able to seize it. It is important to be aware of this issue, and to ensure that your Insolvency Practitioner concludes the IVA quickly.

When an IVA is concluded, the debtor experiences a mixture of emotions and a sharply defined change in circumstances. On the one hand, you will be debt free for the first time in many years. There is no longer anyone to hassle you for money, and this can be a strange experience. Sometimes it can actually be hard to deal with, since the removal of such familiar pressure leaves a substantial gap behind. Whereas the debtor has previously been accustomed to spending a certain degree of mental energy on worrying about debt and struggling to cope with it, suddenly all this is removed. At this point it is important to keep one's feet on the ground; it can be tempting to get another credit card and simply re-offend, as despite all the suffering associated with debt in the past, the debtor often feels a sense of reliance on the stress of unmanageable debt. In a bizarre way, you can become dependent on the adrenaline rush.

On the other hand, even after the IVA has finished there may be some consequences. If you are a homeowner, then you will be left without any available equity in your property, and after the equity release you may be on a more expensive mortgage. Your credit rating will have been damaged by the IVA, and will remain in this state for another twelve months before it starts to repair. This means that it is not possible to effect a 'quick break' at the end of the IVA period, as elements of the IVA are still present in your life for a good while longer. This overhanging shadow can sometimes temper the positive aspects to the IVA, and can take a good deal of getting used to.

My Story

After my IVA had been running for three whole years, due to a stroke of luck my house rose in value and I was able to remortgage it. My Insolvency Practitioner managed to negotiate an early settlement of the IVA using my equity release, which was to the value of twenty-three thousand pounds. Suddenly that was it – game over.

All that remained was for the Insolvency Practitioner to officially conclude the IVA and send us our certificates of completion. But for some reason this didn't happen for three months! I now know that most Insolvency Practitioners seek to conclude IVAs much sooner than that. What this highlights is a point that I keep coming back to: research your Insolvency Practitioner thoroughly, and make absolutely sure that you find the right person for the job before you sign up with them.

Nevertheless, when my IVA was finally concluded, I was so overjoyed – my paycheck came in and all the money was mine to spend, every last penny, without the creditors getting their hands on any of it. It was an exhilarating moment. The first thing that I did was to go out and buy some clothes for my family. It felt like such an extravagant thing to do, as we had not bought any nice clothes for more than three years. The strange thing is that even as I handed over the plastic – it was a debit card, obviously, not a credit card – I had a feeling deep down that this was a wrong, bad thing to do. Over the period of the IVA I had become so conditioned to tight budgeting that when the IVA finished I actually found it difficult to spend normally again.

Yet despite this feeling of guilt associated with spending money, I felt in some way compelled to spend a lot in the weeks following the conclusion of the IVA. It was as if part of me felt that I deserved to indulge myself after such an extended period of frugality, while the other part of me was shocked at the waste of money. This, in a sense, is a good illustration of what it is like to finish the IVA. You are overwhelmed by a mixture of emotions, from an extreme sense of relief to a deep-seated feeling of guilt associated with money.

It is easy to underestimate the pressure that an IVA can put you under, and the turbulence of being released from it. When an IVA comes to an end the debtor does not phase out the payments; they simply stop, from one month to the next. This can be a very sudden transition. In my experience the period following the conclusion of the IVA can be compared to a convict being released from prison; often they have become so accustomed to functioning within the structure of the prison that they are unable to cope with life outside, and re-offend soon after their release. There are no statistics available for the amount of debtors who 're-offend' having gone through an IVA, but I do believe that this is a real danger.

Getting into debt in the first place provides a certain kind of adrenaline rush, and then living within the financial structure of an IVA lends a certain sense of order to one's life. These two factors combined can become an explosive cocktail, once the constraints of the IVA are lifted and the financial horizon widens again; you can feel like a coiled spring that has suddenly been set free. To make matters worse, if you are a homeowner you will find yourself the owner of a property devoid of significant equity. This can cause feelings of frustration and resentment to build up towards your creditors; it can feel as if they have 'robbed' you of all of your financial security. In a similar vein, when your IVA comes to an end you still need to suffer another twelve months of a damaged credit rating. This can cause you to feel as if the IVA is 'lingering', and many people find this state of affairs frustrating. This sense of anger can sometimes cause people to behave recklessly, and exacerbates the danger of impulsive spending sprees. This must be avoided at all costs.

The best advice for getting through this period is to take things slowly and gently. Try to resist the temptation to go out on a 'splurge'. If you want to, treat yourself to a nice dinner in a restaurant or a trip to the cinema, but don't go overboard. Allow yourself to go through a period of re-adjustment, and keep as flexible as possible. Don't beat yourself up for spending money, but don't be reckless with your cash either. Try not to apply for any further credit for as long as possible; I would suggest a year at the very least. In this sense, your damaged credit rating may be more of a blessing than a curse.

Keep telling yourself that there is no need to spend all your extra money at once, there is time to spend it in a sensible manner, and on things you really need. Gradually the transition period will pass, and you will be in a stable financial position; then you will look back and be grateful that you managed to get yourself out of the hole with the aid of the IVA. You will be rehabilitated as a spender, having gained money management skills that are far beyond those of most people, and will feel a definite sense of satisfaction and order in your life. This has got to be the best part of the IVA journey.

IVA.co.uk Forum Members' Stories

Dominic Corby, London

'To my delight, I never had the slightest problem with my Insolvency Practitioner from the beginning of the IVA process until the end. My provider worked very quickly, and to get from the initial phone to the creditors' meeting took just six weeks. My Insolvency Practitioner was easily available, and from the beginning I could see that he was knowledgeable and confident of success. I felt that I was in safe hands, even though I never had a face-to-face meeting with the Insolvency Practitioner.'

'Throughout the IVA I contacted my Insolvency Practitioner by either phone or email and always had a prompt response. When the IVA was finished I was not even aware that some people experience delays in getting their certificate of completion; mine was issued within a couple of weeks. On the whole I am extremely happy with my experience, and feel fortunate that I chose the right IP.'

IVA.co.uk Forum Experts' Advice

Melanie Giles
Melanie Giles is an independent Insolvency Practitioner and has been working in the debt solutions industry for over twenty years.

'You should expect your Insolvency Practitioner to close the case for you as soon as possible. Insolvency Practitioners can, on occasion, be somewhat inefficient and as a client there is not too much you can do about it apart from chasing them regularly. Personally I have a rule where I don't pay myself until the case is closed, to give me and my team an incentive to do it as soon as possible. It might be worth discussing the strategy for concluding the IVA right at the beginning when you are still deciding which Insolvency Practitioner to commit to. Even though it seems a long way away, it is an important issue and you may thank yourself one day for bringing it up.'

Mark Allen

Mark Allen is a partner in the accountancy firm Grant Thornton, and is responsible for the National IVA Service Line. He is a chartered accountant, licensed Insolvency Practitioner and a regular panel member on the televised IVA.co.uk Debates.

'At all times, from the point of view of the Insolvency Practitioner, customer service is paramount. Insolvency Practitioners have a great deal of power over their clients' quality of life, and they do have a duty of care to them throughout the IVA period. From the client's point of view, you should be able to get a feel for the quality of the Insolvency Practitioner's customer relations from your initial dealings with them. While it can often be the case that they put a special effort in when touting for new business, if there are bad tendencies running through the company they should become apparent fairly early on. If you have any concerns, see if there is any feedback about them on the Internet forums.'

Essential Advice

- Discuss and plan the end of your IVA during one of the initial meetings with your Insolvency Practitioner.
- If there is a delay in getting your certificate of completion, chase your Insolvency Practitioner regularly and be aware of your rights.
- Treat yourself once the IVA has finished, but don't be reckless. Avoid taking out credit wherever possible.
- Get in the habit of saving the money that was previously being spent on the IVA each month to build up your savings.

Conclusion

Even though my IVA was a long and difficult journey, ultimately it was worth it. Not only does the IVA give you a chance to put your debts behind you, it rehabilitates you at the same time. You just don't want to go back to the way things were, so you totally change your lifestyle. I am not materialistic any more. I am just not interested in a big house or a flashy car; the Mercedes that I used to own seems totally absurd to me now. The only thing I am interested in is the next family holiday, spending time with my kids, running my shop, and having a peaceful life.

I pay every single bill the very next day. Whereas I used to always be at least four to six weeks behind, now I pay for things as I get them. I save the money that used to go towards paying my IVA. I always think extremely carefully about what I am spending. I wouldn't say that I am miserly; it's just that I am careful about what we buy. Recently we did up the bathroom, top to bottom, for the princely sum of £150! That gave me a terrific sense of achievement. I enjoyed getting the bargains and making sure that it was all done with the absolute minimum of waste. I did the work myself, too, which was a really satisfying experience. And I saved myself hundreds and hundreds of pounds to use on other things. In the past I would have got a decorator in to do it, and I would have ended up spending £2,000. So the IVA has changed me, and I am a better man as a result. I hope that you are able to learn from my mistakes and go into the IVA with your eyes open – and I very much hope it works for you.

The IVA world is changing all the time, but the main principles of taking your head out the sand as soon as possible, researching different companies carefully, and keeping on top of your budget will always remain the same. And as the months go by the industry gets more and more difficult; an increasing number of rogue companies are springing up all the time, and the creditors are in general getting stricter with their requirements. It's not all bad news – there are some great IVA companies out there, and new legislation is being passed regularly to make sure that the IVA marketplace remains fair. Above all, through sources like IVA.co.uk, ordinary people are much more informed about the debt industry, and are better able to make the right decision to find their way out of debt.

Nobody will ever tell you that an IVA is easy. But by following the advice in this book, and making good use of the IVA.co.uk community forum, I can guarantee that you are giving yourself the very best chance of success.

Glossary

(Undischarged) Bankrupt: Someone against whom a Bankruptcy order has been made and who has not been discharged from Bankruptcy.

Bankruptcy: A process whereby debtors declare themselves unable to pay their debts and surrender any valuable assets. The bankrupt will be under certain restrictions for the duration of their Bankruptcy.

Bankruptcy Order: The court order making an individual bankrupt, an individual can petition for their own Bankruptcy, or a creditor can petition for a debtor to be made bankrupt.

Charging Order: A court order placing restrictions on the disposal of certain assets, such as property or securities, given after judgment. It gives priority of payment over other creditors.

Citizens Advice Bureau (CAB): This organisation offers free debt advice and free assistance with setting up Debt Management Plans. However, they can't set up IVAs.

Company Voluntary Arrangement (CVA): A voluntary agreement for a company is a procedure whereby a plan of reorganization or composition in satisfaction of debts is put forward to creditors and shareholders. There is limited involvement by the court and the scheme is under the control of a Supervisor.

Consolidation Loan: A loan that is taken out to pay off multiple debts. It may be secured or unsecured, and is typically used to pay off high interest debts like credit cards, replacing them with a single debt with a lower rate of interest.

Consumer Credit Counselling Service: This is a charity funded by the banks which sets up Debt Management Plans for free.

Creditor: These are the people you owe money to. If the debt is linked to your house, for example a mortgage or secured loan, the creditors are called 'secured creditors'. These people can't be paid off through an IVA because if you are insolvent they can simply seize your house. If the debt is not linked to your house, for example a credit card or unsecured loan, the creditors are called 'unsecured creditors'. These debts can be dealt with through an IVA.

Debt Adviser: These are the people you would usually speak to first when researching debt solutions. A good debt adviser will talk you through all the options available to you so that the best option naturally becomes apparent. Beware unscrupulous debt advisers who demand large upfront fees or try to steer you towards one solution in particular without listening to you properly. Your debt adviser should be knowledgeable, objective and clear in the way they explain the options to you. Their initial advice should always be provided for free.

Debt Management Plan Companies: These companies don't provide IVAs. They provide Debt Management Plans. A Debt

Management Plan is not legally binding like an IVA, and does not write off debt. It simply reduces the amount you pay each month, but extends the length of time you pay it for. The DMP Company will negotiate with creditors to reduce your monthly payments. They would also strive to persuade the creditors to freeze interest and charges for up to one year at a time.

Debtor: That's the person who borrowed the money. It is important to remember that from a legal point of view the debtor is the person whose name is on the form and who signed the dotted line. So even if you borrowed money on someone else's behalf, if the debt is in your name you are the debtor and the buck stops with you.

Dividend: This is the amount that a debtor offers to repay through an IVA. For example, if an IVA proposes to repay £25,000 from total debts of £50,000, that would be a dividend of 50p in the pound, or 50% of the overall debt.

Hurdle Rate: Some creditors have their own hurdle rates – the minimum amount they want to be repaid, for example 40p in the pound, before they will vote in favour of an IVA.

Individual Voluntary Arrangement (IVA): A Voluntary Arrangement for an individual is a procedure whereby the person comes to an arrangement of compromise with creditors as to how their debt will be discharged, typically by five years of monthly payments. Such a scheme requires the approval of the court and is under the control of a supervisor.

Insolvent: The state of not being able to pay ones debts as they fall due, or having an excess of liabilities over assets.

Insolvency Act 1986: Legislation governing insolvency law and practice. Many other statutes and statutory instruments are also relevant.

Insolvency Practitioner (IP): This is the person who will draft your final IVA proposal, negotiate it with your creditors, and supervise your arrangement throughout the IVA period.

Interim Order: An individual who intends to propose an IVA to his/her creditors may, if necessary, apply to the court for an interim order which, if granted, precludes Bankruptcy and other legal proceedings whilst the order is in force.

Preferential Creditor: Has priority when funds are distributed by a liquidator, administrative receiver or trustee in Bankruptcy.

Proof of Debt: The document submitted in an insolvency to establish a creditor's claim. It may be informal (e.g. by letter) or in a prescribed form.

Receiver: The person appointed by the court for some specific purpose or the person appointed by a mortgage to exercise his rights over the charge's property under the Law of Property Act 1925 (not to be confused with the Official Receiver or Administrative Receiver).

Receivership: The general term applied when a person is appointed as a receiver or administrative receiver over certain assets.

Secured Creditor: A creditor with specific rights over some or all of a debtor's assets in the event of insolvency. In essence, they are paid first from the secured assets.

Supervisor: The person appointed to supervise the implementation of the debtor's proposals for an IVA or CVA once approved by creditors (and members). This person is usually the Insolvency Practitioner (IP).

Transaction at an Undervalue: A transaction at an undervalue can describe either a gift or a transaction in which the consideration received is significantly less than that given.

Trustee: In Bankruptcy: the authorized Insolvency Practitioner appointed to deal with the estate of the bankrupt. Under a deed of arrangement: the authorized Insolvency Practitioner appointed to deal with the estate of the person who entered into the deed.

Unsecured Creditor: Strictly, any creditor who does not hold security. More commonly used to refer to any ordinary creditor who has no preferential rights, although, in fact preferential creditors will almost always also be unsecured.

www.ingramcontent.com/pod-product-compliance
Ingram Content Group UK Ltd.
Pitfield, Milton Keynes, MK11 3LW, UK
UKHW041437180426
11947UKWH00007B/487